# RETRO RECIPES

BOBBY HICKS

Vintage Dishes *with* *a* Modern Twist

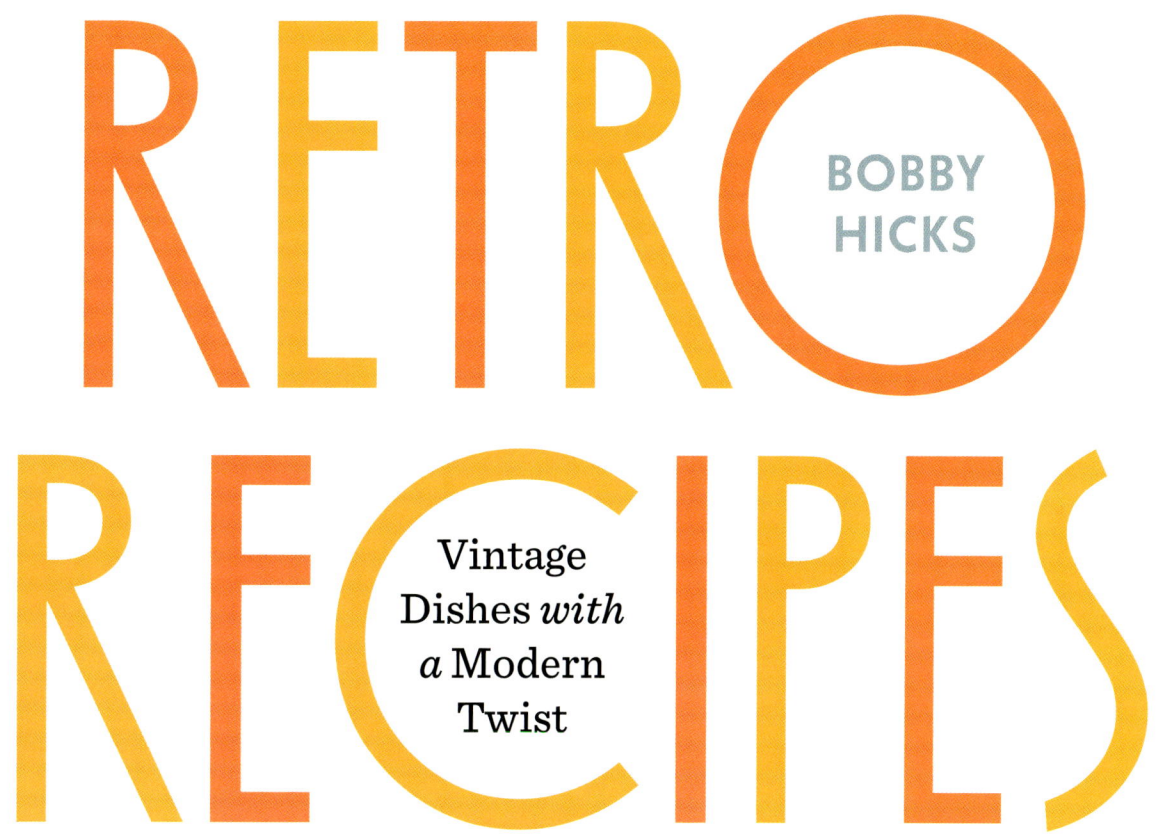

**Countryman Press**

*An Imprint of W. W. Norton & Company*
*Independent Publishers Since 1923*

Copyright © 2026 by Robert Hicks II
Photographs © 2026 by Keiko Groves
Illustrations © 2026 by Brandon Campbell

All rights reserved
Printed in China
First Edition

For information about permission to reproduce selections from this book, write to Permissions, Countryman Press, 500 Fifth Avenue, New York, NY 10110

For information about special discounts for bulk purchases, please contact W. W. Norton Special Sales at specialsales@wwnorton.com or 800-233-4830

Manufacturing by RRD Asia
Book design by Raphael Geroni
Art director: Allison Chi
Production manager: Devon Zahn

Library of Congress Cataloging-in-Publication Data is available.

ISBN 978-1-324-11725-4

Countryman Press
www.countrymanpress.com

An imprint of W. W. Norton & Company, Inc.
500 Fifth Avenue, New York, NY 10110
www.wwnorton.com

Authorized EU representative: EAS, Mustamäe tee 50, 10621 Tallinn, Estonia

1 2 3 4 5 6 7 8 9 0

*To my parents and my partner, Keiko*
*For always believing in me and*
*for showing me the right paths*

# CONTENTS

## BREADS & SANDWICHES

## MEATS

## ❋ POULTRY ❋

## ❖ SEAFOOD ❖

## ❄ BEVERAGES ❄

## ❖ SWEETS, CAKES & PIES ❖

## ❋ ESSENTIALS, EXTRAS & EVERYDAY SKILLS ❋

# INTRODUCTION

**WHENEVER** people ask me why I got into cooking, they seem somewhat disappointed to learn that I don't have a charming backstory like someone who stood beside their grandmother in the kitchen, kneading dough and picking fresh herbs. I never had the childhood passion to open *Mastering the Art of French Cooking* by Julia Child at nine years old, or to rush home after school to watch Jacques Pépin discuss the beauty of an onion—this all came much later in my life. As a child, I was too busy eating snack cakes, climbing trees, and playing hide-and-seek while wearing my mom's expensive mud mask as camouflage.

I grew up on a small farm in central Florida with a stay-at-home mother who gave horse-back riding lessons and a father who was an orthodontist. My mom cooked simple meals she had learned as an adult, but those meals never inspired me to want to become a cook—and they often lacked seasoning. It wasn't until I was a young teenager, while my dad was trying to cook pork chops, that I realized two things: He couldn't cook to save his life and, if I wanted to eat food that wasn't burnt to a crisp, I'd need to learn how to fend for myself.

When we start cooking, we often gravitate toward meals that bring us joy, serving as our guiding star—our starting point. For me, breakfast quickly became, and will likely always be, one of my favorite things to cook. After watching my mom cook breakfast, I would grab some bacon and add it to a pan, watching it crisp up (or burn—don't do that), and I'd explore the delicacy and versatility of eggs: frying, scrambling,

and even learning how to boil them hard. As a sixteen-year-old, I felt excited to cook, but it wasn't a passionate pursuit; I was just curious.

My curiosity, as I came to realize, wasn't limited to food. I found myself exploring a dozen or more interests simultaneously, absorbing information and learning quickly. Guitars and music were prominent in my home, so I started a band. I enjoyed being active outdoors, leading me to take up cross-country running, where I spent hours each week practicing my gait and stride to improve my split times. My best friend, Billy, wanted to get a tattoo for his eighteenth birthday, so I dedicated countless hours at the tattoo shop, asking questions and learning. I was hungry for knowledge, casting a wide net and taking in whatever I could.

Years later, I learned more about ADHD and how it likely fit into the narrative of my life. I began to understand that I wasn't an "idiot," as many kids had assumed; I just lacked the tools to focus and hone my attention. However, when something piqued my interest, I would become engrossed in it, often ending up knowing more than most about a particular topic. This hyperfixation later became my superpower, allowing me to memorize recipes, historical facts, and the names and dates of people from a hundred years ago.

After a short stint in college (wasn't for me), I was twenty-one years old and working as a delivery driver for Domino's Pizza. My friend (and eventual partner), Keiko, decided to move to Brooklyn. She's the most self-motivated person I know and always inspired me to push myself to be better, work harder, so I decided that I wanted to follow her there. It turned out to be the best decision I've ever made. I had saved about $6,000, but needed to save more. I started to buy groceries and cook my meals instead of eating out every day. For $25, I could buy a large bag of frozen tilapia at Walmart along with some packages of frozen cheesy rice and broccoli (today this same trip might cost over $100), and I routinely cooked this meal for months until I mastered it. For the first time in my life, I had a reason to cook, and it grew on me. I enjoyed the warmth of the old electric oven and the timing involved in plating my meals to ensure I wouldn't be eating cold food. I experimented with seasonings, acid, and texture and felt an unexpected interest blossom. The seed had been planted, and I was eager to learn more.

A few months later, I bought a one-way plane ticket to New York City and boarded with just a small suitcase of clothing and a backpack. I had no practical work experience beyond delivering pizza or making someone a coffee, but I was determined to make this move work. When I landed, Keiko already had a list of places that I could visit for open-call applications, and I hit the ground running. Within my first week in Brooklyn, I found a job as a room server at the beautiful Soho Grand Hotel, where I worked for over three years.

I worked the breakfast shift, waking up around 3 a.m. most days so I could shower, hop on the train, and get into the city before 5 a.m. The room service staff worked out of the kitchen, which was complete with rubber mats to prevent slipping and the ubiquitous aroma of spices, herbs, and aromatics like shallots and garlic, gently sautéing in a large rondeau on one of the burners. I spent hours observing the kitchen staff, timidly making notes about ingredients that I'd never heard of and writing down words

like "tartare" to look them up later. Eventually, I got to know everyone well enough to start asking questions.

"Hey, Hugo, why are you putting that omelet in the oven? Doesn't it cook on the stovetop?"

"Mackie, what's that yellow stuff you're whisking, and why is the metal bowl over that pot of boiling water?"

"Andrew, what's the difference between an omelet and a frittata?" (Mind you, I had never even heard the word "frittata" before this place.)

I learned something new every day, and I was getting paid to do it! But everything changed for me when a new executive chef, Paul, arrived at the hotel.

One day, while I was filling a tumbler of coffee for a guest and waiting for the last order of French toast to be made for breakfast, I asked Tommy, the senior breakfast cook, how they made the compound butter served on top of the toast. He explained that they used a stand mixer to combine the butter with zest from oranges and lemons, along with some juice, then chilled it all in a mold. I tucked this valuable information away and delivered the guest's meal, only to find Chef Paul approaching me. Large and (literally) in charge, he asked why I was talking to the cooks instead of him, the head chef.

This was my moment—a moment that possibly changed my life. I asked Paul how I could work with him after my shift ended. I told him I didn't even need to be paid; I just wanted to learn how to cook. He took me to the hotel's Human Resources department, and for the next year, I volunteered countless hours after working long shifts in room service. I pushed myself to learn as much as I could. Was I holding the knife properly? Were my cuts precise? Was I working quickly and cleanly enough? I was always in my head, striving to improve so my peers would respect me—and it paid off.

When Chef Paul left the hotel, I stopped cooking in the kitchen. The next chef didn't share the same enthusiasm and wasn't interested in having a rookie take up space; he didn't see what Paul saw in me. But my path didn't end there—it had only just begun. The bar manager, Kevin, invited me to transfer to his team as a barback. I spent eight months changing kegs and filling ice bins on busy weekends until 2 a.m. My schedule shifted entirely; I became a night owl again, like I was when I was younger. I started slowly, but I worked hard to show Kevin the same energy I had shown Chef Paul, and eventually, I established myself as an excellent bartender. I memorized hundreds of cocktail recipes and their histories.

During those years, I was always juggling two or three jobs to make ends meet. While I was working my second job as a host at an outdoor dining patio at the Standard Hotel one evening, Chef Paul showed up, dressed in a leather jacket to fend off the brisk Manhattan breeze of fall.

"Bobby, I came to make this quick," he said as I offered him a table. "I can't stay long, but I came to tell you that you're quitting your job and coming to cook with me down the street at Soho House. Give your two weeks' notice, and then we'll get you set up."

My heart stopped, but I felt a sense of relief and calm. Without missing a beat, I shook his hand, wished him well, and immediately submitted my notice to my manager, who was heartbroken, as he had been about to promote me to floor manager. "I'm sorry, brother. Destiny awaits," I said.

For the next year and a half, I was challenged daily, working twelve- to fifteen-hour shifts, where I began with the prep cooks, moved to the line, and eventually ran the banquet department, handling several dinner parties each day, cooking for anywhere from five to fifty people.

Eventually, Paul left, and I followed suit. I realized that I was happier when I was working as a bartender because I loved talking to people! I decided to fully commit to bartending, and found a job working at the Meatball Shop with Jason Cousins, the bartender who had trained me at the Soho Grand Hotel. It was casual and loud, and though we did pride ourselves on our beverage program, I wanted something more.

Not long after, I was introduced to Theo Lieberman, the principal bartender at Lantern's Keep, a midtown Manhattan cocktail bar in the Iroquois Hotel, while doing my own research on what a *real* cocktail bar did. I had walked over to Raines Law Room, a speakeasy near the Union Square Market, dressed in my trademark button-up shirt, tie, and suspenders, and saw the barman, Jesse.

"What can I get for you, sir?" he asked.

"Bartender's choice," I said, giving a quiet nod and taking in the atmosphere. I *loved* it.

Several moments later, he returned with a martini variation that I had never tried but had read about called the Poet's Dream—a gin martini with a hint of Bénédictine.

"Here you go, sir," Jesse said, carefully sliding the martini coup in front of me. "The Poet's Dream. You *do* know what this is, right?"

My heart sank, feeling the judgment. I acknowledged that "of course" I knew what it was, even noting that I had read it was from the 1940s. Jesse looked over toward a very young, skinny guy with glasses and both gave a snicker. I had had enough. I drank the drink, left the cash, and stood up to leave, feeling foolish for trying to fit in. And just before I could leave the stool, the young man stopped me and struck up a conversation.

"Where do you work?" he asked. "You know your stuff, it seems!"

"In Brooklyn," I said, knowing that if they didn't think I was an embarrassment already, they would when they found out I worked at a place that specialized in meatball smash sandwiches and slinging drinks instead of creating sophisticated cocktails.

"Well, here's my card," he said. "If you're ever interested in working uptown, let me know." The business card was simple: "Theo Lieberman. Principal Barman. Lantern's Keep."

Once again, an opportunity presented itself, and I took it. Within two weeks, I was working at LK, as we called it, and also working at the Meatball Shop. It didn't take long before I was setting up, breaking down, and running my shifts, taking care of my guests, and becoming the person that even Theo came to about cocktails.

Lantern's Keep was a sister bar to the world-famous Milk & Honey, located on the Lower East Side and one of the most beloved cocktail bars in the country. Theo also worked shifts there when he wasn't working with me at LK, so when Milk & Honey relocated to the Flatiron District, I was asked to join the team. There was no menu at Milk & Honey; everyone who worked there was a bartender. We alternated shifts between floor work and making drinks, asking patrons about their favorite spirits, whether they wanted something shaken with citrus or stirred and boozy, and if they preferred something tall with soda water or served up in a martini coupe. At this point, my ADHD hyperfixation truly shined.

My drinks were published in *The New York Times*, and I began gaining a reputation among the bartenders in the city. I started to receive recognition not just locally, but also nationally as I explored the up-and-coming platform, Instagram. There, I rekindled my love for photography with Keiko, and we spent our free time traveling around the tri-state area, capturing stunning and aspirational photographs by mountainsides and in forests ablaze with autumn's orange and red hues. People responded well to our content, but everything changed when the landlord decided to sell the building, leading to the closure of Milk & Honey. This change opened up a new path for me.

I was no longer cooking or bartending, but I discovered a similar hyperfixation and passion for photography and videography. I invested money—some that I didn't have—into better cameras, lighting, and audio equipment. I learned to edit videos and even made a living for a while shooting weddings. Although things were progressing, I felt something was missing.

For more than eight years, I poured my energy into content creation, constantly striving to surpass other creators. I began to gamify my work to keep pace with the growing pressures of a changing algorithm, resulting in frequent burnout. Nothing seemed enjoyable, and I often felt like a fraud. Then, in March 2020, the world came to a halt due to the COVID-19 pandemic. For the first time, I was confined to my small apartment, unable to explore, socialize, or satisfy my creative urges. That was undoubtedly one of the hardest years for me; I felt truly lost, but it also forced me to reflect on myself and adapt.

By the end of the year, Keiko and I were fortunate enough to buy our first home in the small town of Coconut Creek, Florida, where she grew up. We moved closer to her family, and I finally found the opportunity to combine my skills and create the content I had always wanted to produce. In April 2021, I shared my first Retro Rec-

ipes Kitchen video, cooking "Bunny Biscuits" from *Betty Crocker's New Boys and Girls Cookbook*. I was hooked.

Making these videos provided everything I needed for my dopamine-depleted brain—it allowed me to be creative, explore recipes, and learn food history. What started as a fun hobby soon transformed into my passion, and I realized that I was finally doing what I was meant to do.

The Japanese word *ikigai* refers to an occupation that gives life meaning. It encompasses what you love, what you're good at, what the world needs, and what you can be paid to do. There has never been a word more perfectly crafted to describe my experience. Although I found joy in cooking with Chef Paul and bartending alongside some of the best bartenders in the country, creating Retro Recipes Kitchen has given me a joy that only comes from doing something that truly belongs to yourself.

For nearly five years, I've dedicated countless hours to creating content, exploring food history, researching, and filming videos for others' entertainment. It has brought me immense pleasure, even during exhausting or overwhelming times. This platform has allowed me to set my own hours and taught me more through practical experience than any culinary school ever could. And now, it has given me the incredible opportunity to write this book for you.

I could never have imagined the journey that lies ahead of me, but that's the enchanting aspect of destiny: You never know where it will lead you. However, if you're willing to put in the effort, embrace the opportunities, and step into the unknown, you'll likely be pleased with what you discover on the other side. Whether you're in search of beautiful breads, comforting casseroles, or perfect pies, I believe there's something for everyone in this book.

# WHAT ARE RETRO RECIPES?

**WHEN** I ask people what comes to mind when they think of "retro recipes," the first things I hear are Jell-O, boxed mixes, canned soups, and tinned meats and fish—and they wouldn't be wrong. When I think of a retro recipe, I consider the nostalgia that these dishes or ingredients evoke. For the last five or more years, I have said that my brand isn't recreating weird or silly dishes—my brand is recreating nostalgia.

From my years of exploration, cooking through hundreds of recipes, I have found many dishes that indeed fit the bill of an entrée entirely created from canned products or some struggle-bus desserts made from unexpected ingredients (*tomato soup cake, anyone?*). Though they typically lacked adventure, seasoning, or excitement, they provided essential nourishment for families and friends, which was more than enough at the time. It's only when you take a step back and look at the timeline of American cuisine that the pieces seem to make sense. The turn of the last century wasn't known for blowing the roof off with culinary masterpieces, but there was a fundamental understanding of the need to learn *how* to cook.

Through my research, I discovered that many of these seemingly bizarre or unappetizing dishes, like sweetbread pie or tongue sandwiches, could actually be quite decent—if not absolutely delicious—when made with a bit more technique and a lot more seasoning. Whenever possible, I opted to make my own sauces and bases instead of relying on canned soups. If a recipe called for a can of corn, I would seek out fresh summer corn in season. And if a dish suggested using $\frac{1}{8}$ teaspoon of salt, I'd ignore that and cook intuitively, relying on my taste buds to create a well-seasoned meal suited for modern palates.

We often perceive the mid-twentieth century and earlier as a dark age of food history, but my hope for this book is to provide insight into why food was prepared the way it was. In *Retro Recipes*, we'll explore the good, the bad, and the gelatin, updating every recipe for today's tastes.

Each recipe will include volumetric measurements, such as cups and tablespoons, as well as grams and ounces, making it easier for you to approach these dishes however you prefer to cook. But throughout this book, please remember this essential principle: Cook with your heart.

These recipes represent years of note-taking, testing, and refining, created just for this moment. My personal preferences may not reflect yours. Feel free to substitute ingredients based on your tastes or dietary restrictions. And above all, cook this food in a way that appeals to you—because when you're happy with your cooking, everyone else will be, too.

As you read *Retro Recipes*, you'll journey through a progression of recipes, some dating all the way back to the fifteenth and sixteenth centuries. Each chapter offers a snapshot of tasty treats and savory bites that satiated and nourished lives for nearly a century or more. So, wash your hands, clean your countertop, and let's get ready to dine through the decades!

# STARTERS, GREENS & THINGS

**ENTERTAINING** and cooking for guests has been a celebrated tradition around the world throughout much of human history. Caring for others and sharing food is one of the most personal and rewarding things you can do. Whether you're quickly microwaving snacks on a paper plate for game day or carefully plating canapés for an elegant gathering, the same love and effort are involved, regardless of the final presentation.

The starters in this book are some of my favorites because they reflect how we celebrated entertaining during the 1950s and 1960s, with loud, colorful, and sometimes absurd bites of food that were filled with love (and possibly cigarette ash). Lavish parties with exotic themes, costumes, and specially designed menus transported guests to different times and places—an idea widely promoted in cookbooks, magazines, and popular television shows. The mid-century period was largely focused on status, and when you make

entertaining a game, it results in some truly memorable hors d'oeuvres.

If I'm being honest, I'm still not convinced that the mid-century truly understood what a salad is, as many of the "salad" recipes in my collection of cookbooks are gelatin-based monstrosities. To avoid any confusion, I'm simply referring to this chapter as "Starters, Greens & Things" because most of the recipes here are vegetarian or primarily vegetable-focused. I can't, in good conscience, call a Jell-O dish a salad.

I believe there's something for everyone in this chapter. I've made it a point to improve upon each of the dishes in some way, incorporating flavor, spice, or new techniques to create meals you'd be happy to share with family and friends. I'm hoping to present vibrant and visually striking dishes ideal for fun, retro-themed parties, along with simple, delicious, and crave-worthy starters—and wiggly things—that have been enjoyed throughout the decades.

# HOPPIN' JOHN

HOPPIN' John, a dish made of peas and rice, has deep roots in American history, dating back well before the 1900s. It was first introduced by the Gullah people of Lowcountry South Carolina. Pigeon peas, also known as black-eyed peas, were originally brought from West Africa to the United States during the slave trade. For centuries, this dish has been served on New Year's Day to bring prosperity and romance in the coming year. It is commonly served with collard greens, cornbread, and ribs.

The origin of the name "hoppin' John" is somewhat unclear, much like many recipes in this book. However, a popular theory suggests that it is derived from the French term for pigeon peas, *pois pigeon*, which is pronounced "pwah pee-jon" and sounds a lot like "hoppin' John" when spoken quickly. ✦ *Makes 10 servings*

4 tablespoons (56 g) unsalted butter
1 onion, diced
1 large carrot, diced
2 celery stalks, diced
1 ham hock
5 cups (1.2 L) Homemade Chicken Stock (page 225)

1 pound (450 g) dried black-eyed peas, soaked overnight and drained
Salt and ground black pepper to taste
1 teaspoon (2 g) cayenne pepper
2 tablespoons (30 mL) apple cider vinegar
3 cups (600 g) white rice, cooked
Minced fresh chives, for garnish (optional)

1. In a large, heavy-bottomed pot or Dutch oven, melt the butter over medium heat. Add the onion, carrot, and celery and sweat the vegetables for 5 to 10 minutes, stirring occasionally.

2. Add the ham hock and chicken stock, cover, and cook for 2 hours.

3. Remove the ham hock, pull the meat off, and roughly chop it, then return the meat to the pot (discard the bone). Add the black-eyed peas. Cover and cook over medium heat for 45 to 60 minutes, or until the peas are tender.

4. If there is too much liquid, turn the heat down to medium-low and continue to cook gently with the lid off to evaporate some of the stock.

5. Season with salt and black pepper to taste, then add the cayenne and apple cider vinegar to help balance the richness of the pork.

6. Either serve the peas on top of the cooked rice or add the white rice to the pot to serve them mixed together. Garnish with chives if desired.

**NOTE:** *There are many variations of hoppin' John that use other vegetables or even different peas, so feel free to experiment. To make this dish vegetarian, you can omit the ham hock; use vegetable stock instead of chicken stock and add 1 teaspoon smoked paprika to replace the deep, smoky taste that the ham hock adds to the dish.*

# VICHYSSOISE

ONE of Julia Child's favorite meals, vichyssoise was created in 1917 at the Ritz-Carlton hotel in Manhattan by the renowned French chef Louis Diat. He developed this cold potato and leek soup as a tribute to a recipe his grandmother would make during his childhood. According to legend, Diat began cooling his potato and leek soup with chilled milk because he enjoyed the flavor, and this practice became a staple of the dish. ✦ *Makes 10 servings*

3 cups (450 g) peeled and diced Yukon
    Gold potatoes
3 cups (750 g) sliced leek whites
6 cups (1.5 L) Homemade Chicken Stock
    (page 225)

1 cup (240 mL) heavy cream
Salt and ground white pepper to taste
5 tablespoons (15 g) minced fresh chives

1. Add the potatoes, leeks, and chicken stock to a large, heavy-bottomed pot or Dutch oven and simmer over medium heat for 30 to 40 minutes, or until the potatoes are fork-tender.

2. Working in batches as necessary, transfer everything to a blender and puree into a rich, creamy soup. (Alternatively, you can use an immersion blender right in the pot.)

3. Return the soup to the pot and add the cream. Season with salt and white pepper to taste.

4. Serve with a generous portion of minced chives.

**NOTES:** *Less is more with this gorgeous soup, but if you feel like adding some texture, I'd encourage the addition of croutons or even crispy bacon crumbles at serving time.*

*If you do not have leeks, use onions! To make it vegetarian, use vegetable stock instead of chicken stock.*

# BISCUITS and SORGHUM

ONE of the most remarkable people I've ever met was Moe, my partner Keiko's great-grandmother. She lived through some of the most challenging chapters in American history, including the Great Depression. Like many children of that era, she left school early to help support her family, taking a job as a factory seamstress before she ever reached high school. Despite her formal education being cut short, Moe was sharp as a tack. She was brilliant, talented, and endlessly resourceful, with a fiery wit that she carried well into her final days. Even her stories of hardship had a hint of humor: "The Great Depression? Nothing 'great' about it!"

I was fascinated to learn that during those times of food scarcity, she and her family made do with biscuits and sorghum, a molasses-like syrup. It may not sound as interesting as some other dishes, but it's downright heavenly—as long as you're not eating it for breakfast, lunch, and dinner (as Moe would remind you). Sorghum has a lighter yet more complex flavor than cane molasses, and when whipped with heaps of butter, there's nothing better to sop up with a warm biscuit. If you already have it on hand, molasses will do just fine. "Use it up, wear it out. Make it do, or do without."

✦ *Makes 9 biscuits*

**FOR THE DOUGH**
2 cups (240 g) all-purpose flour
2 tablespoons (25 g) sugar (optional)
1 tablespoon (14 g) baking powder
½ teaspoon (3 g) salt
1¼ cups (300 mL) heavy cream, plus
  more for brushing
1 large egg yolk

**FOR SERVING**
Softened butter
Sorghum or molasses
Jam (optional)
Fresh thyme leaves (optional)

1. Preheat the oven to 400°F (200°C) with a rack in the middle position. Line a rimmed baking sheet with parchment paper.

2. Combine the flour, sugar (if making sweet biscuits), baking powder, and salt in a large bowl. Gradually add the cream to the bowl and mix until you have a shaggy dough that is incorporated but not overmixed.

3. Turn the dough out onto a lightly floured surface and roll into a 12-inch square. Using a bench scraper, fold one side inward to the center, then fold the other side to the center, so it becomes a 12 × 6-inch rectangle. Then fold the top edge down to the center, and then the bottom. Now the dough should be roughly a 6-inch square. Dust your hands with some extra flour if needed to prevent stickiness.

4. Gently roll the dough again into a 12-inch square, and repeat the folding process.

*Recipe continues* ➤

5. Gently roll the dough one last time into a 12-inch square and square off the edges. Cut into 9 even biscuits using a knife or bench scraper and cutting straight down.

6. Place the biscuits on the prepared baking sheet, 2 inches apart. In a small bowl, whisk together the egg yolk and 1 to 2 teaspoons heavy cream. Brush the mixture on top of the biscuits.

7. Bake the biscuits until golden brown on top, 12 to 15 minutes. Check after 10 minutes if using convection.

8. Allow to cool on the baking sheet for about 10 minutes, then split the warm biscuits in half and spread with a light smear of softened butter. Spoon a tablespoon of sorghum or molasses on top, along with a bit of jam and thyme, if you like.

NOTES: *You can absolutely use a round cutter for your biscuits, but I prefer the rectangular shape, as it results in less waste and less handling.*

*Avoid "cutting" the dough with a knife, bench scraper, or round cutter—simply press down and lift up. This will prevent crimping the dough, which reduces the rise of the biscuits.*

# The EGG GRAB

DURING the 1930s, rationing and food reserves were common across much of the United States. While the nation was recovering from World War I and emerging from the Roaring Twenties, the stock market crash of 1929 left many Americans in dire circumstances, leading to a widespread need to ration food supplies.

Many men would wake up early and work until sunset, requiring calorie-dense meals that they could easily pack into a container and take with them and eat throughout the day to sustain their energy levels. The egg grab can be seen as one of the first "fast food" meals for those on the go, and it remains delicious even today. ✦ *Makes 4 servings*

3 russet potatoes, peeled and cut into medium dice

4 strips bacon, cut into batons

4 to 6 large eggs, beaten

2 tablespoons (28 g) unsalted butter

2 tablespoons (16 g) all-purpose flour

1½ cups (360 mL) milk, cold

Salt and ground black pepper to taste

¼ teaspoon (0.5 g) cayenne pepper

2 tablespoons (8 g) chopped fresh parsley

1. Bring a large pot of salted water to a boil, tasting the water when warm to ensure it's salty like the sea.

2. Add the potatoes and cook until fork-tender, 12 to 15 minutes. Drain and set aside.

3. Add the bacon to a cold sauté pan with a couple tablespoons of water and heat over medium-high heat. (The water will help render the fat more effectively.) Cook, stirring frequently, until crispy, about 10 minutes. Transfer the bacon to a paper towel–lined plate and pour off all but 1 to 2 tablespoons of the bacon fat from the pan (reserve the bacon fat you're pouring off if you want to use it to cook the roux).

4. Add the cooked potatoes to the hot bacon fat still in the pan and cook, stirring occasionally, until crispy, 8 to 10 minutes. Transfer the potatoes to a bowl.

5. Add the beaten eggs to the pan and cook over low heat, continuously stirring with a silicone spatula to soft-scrambled curds, about 5 minutes. Remove the pan from the heat.

6. In a small saucepan, add the butter or reserved bacon fat and melt over medium heat. Add the flour and whisk for about 5 minutes, or until the roux turns a soft tan color. Add the cold milk and whisk until it thickens into a béchamel. Season with salt and black pepper to taste, then add the cayenne.

7. To assemble, place some fried potatoes on each plate, top with some soft-scrambled eggs, and pour over some béchamel and top with a generous sprinkle of crispy bacon. Garnish with the parsley and serve immediately, while warm.

# DUCHESS SOUP

◇◇◇◇◇◇◇◇◇◇◇◇◇◇◇◇◇◇◇◇◇◇◇ **1930s** ◇◇◇◇◇◇◇◇◇◇◇◇◇

LIKE many of the recipes in this book, duchess soup was either not important enough to record the history of its origin, or it is shrouded in mystery and lore—which is a crime, considering how awesome this simple dish is. When I first came across it, I assumed it would be a bland bowl of soup, but after making it, I was pleasantly surprised! There's something incredibly comforting about the simplicity of this soup. I see it as a fantastic base that can easily be enhanced with any ingredients you want to add.

Instead of using a traditional roux as a thickening agent, this recipe utilizes the robust flavor of salty, buttery crackers, which effectively thickens the soup—it really works!  ✦ *Makes 6 servings*

6 cups (1.4 L) whole milk
½ onion, finely diced
3 tablespoons (42 g) unsalted butter
1 cup (70 g) crushed saltine crackers
½ cup (60 g) shredded cheddar cheese

2 tablespoons (8 g) chopped fresh
    parsley, plus more for garnish
Salt and ground black pepper to taste
Oyster crackers, for serving

1. In a large saucepot, combine the milk and onion and bring to a gentle boil over medium-high heat for just a moment to scald the milk.

2. Turn the heat down to medium, add the butter and crushed crackers, and cook for 5 minutes, or until thickened nicely.

3. Add the cheese and parsley and season to taste.

4. Working in batches as necessary, transfer everything to a blender and puree until smooth.

5. Serve immediately, while warm, garnished with additional parsley and topped with oyster crackers.

**NOTE:** *Feel free to add other ingredients, like cooked bits of meat or seafood. Or treat it like a chowder and add some chopped crispy bacon to amp it up to your taste!*

# CARROT CROQUETTES

GROWING up, I was *not* a fan of leftovers. I was that stubborn kid who felt like I would die if yesterday's dinner touched my plate, as if I were destined to contract a horrible disease. However, as I got older, I began to appreciate the value of a dollar and realized there are many creative ways to reuse food. I discovered that, in fact, I would not die from a plague if I reheated my meatloaf.

This recipe comes from one of my favorite books, *500 Delicious Dishes from Leftovers*, first published in 1941. It's one of my favorite ways to transform almost any leftover into something fresh, delicious, and appealing. ✦ *Makes 6 servings*

### FOR THE CROQUETTES
½ cup (120 g) mashed cooked sweet
    potato
1 cup (100 g) grated carrots
½ shallot, finely minced
1 garlic clove, finely minced
1 tablespoon (15 mL) olive oil
¼ cup (30 g) potato starch
¼ cup (13 g) panko breadcrumbs
¼ cup (16 g) minced fresh parsley
1 large egg yolk
1½ tablespoons (12 g) Madras curry
    powder
1 tablespoon (15 g) salt

### FOR THE BREADING
1 cup (120 g) all-purpose flour
2 teaspoons (10 g) salt
1 teaspoon (2 g) cayenne pepper
3 large eggs
2 cups (100 g) panko breadcrumbs

Vegetable oil, for frying
Kosher salt to taste
Fresh parsley sprigs, for garnish
Calabrian chili sauce or an herby aioli,
    for dipping

1. In a large bowl, combine the sweet potato, carrots, shallot, garlic, olive oil, potato starch, breadcrumbs, parsley, egg yolk, curry powder, and salt. Mix together with a fork, then shape the mixture into six 4-inch "carrots." Place the croquettes on a rimmed baking sheet or large platter and freeze for at least 1 hour to firm up.

2. Prepare a breading station with three shallow dishes. In the first, whisk together the flour, salt, and cayenne. In the second, whisk the eggs. Put the breadcrumbs in the third.

3. Working with one frozen "carrot" at a time, roll it first in the seasoned flour, then transfer to the eggs, then roll it around in the breadcrumbs until it is completely coated. If you see dry spots of white flour after the egg dip, return to the egg dip and coat again. Return the breaded croquettes to the baking sheet.

4. Put the croquettes in the freezer for about 30 minutes to help keep them from falling apart while frying.

*Recipe continues* ➤

5. In a large, heavy-bottomed pot or Dutch oven, add enough oil to deep fry and heat to 375°F (190°C). Line a plate with paper towels. Working in batches, fry the croquettes, flipping every 10 to 20 seconds, for about 5 minutes, or until golden brown and crispy. Using tongs, transfer the fried croquettes to the paper towels and season with a pinch of kosher salt.

6. Arrange the croquettes on a serving platter, radiating from the center, with parsley sprigs at the wide end to resemble carrot tops. Serve with your favorite dipping sauce.

**NOTES:** *These croquettes can be made with almost any other vegetable, such as leftover mashed potatoes. You can even add protein to the croquettes, like yesterday's rotisserie chicken!*

*These are delicious served with Calabrian chilies or other spicy condiments.*

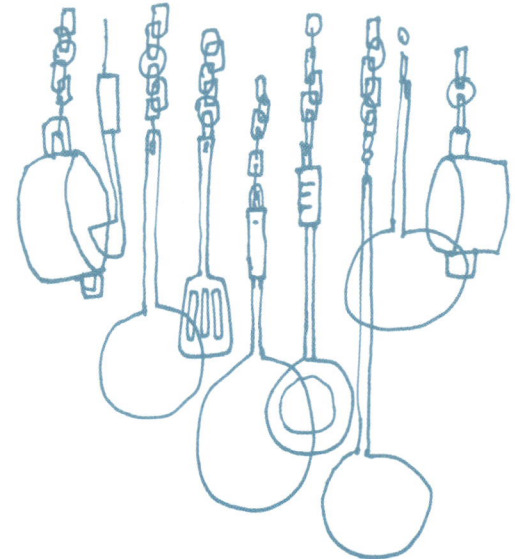

# BURNING BUSH

1950s

ONE of my favorite aspects of the mid-century era is the beautiful ways people prepared their dishes. Ornate shapes, vibrant colors, and layered presentations were common sights at dinner tables, showcasing individual flair in the kitchen.

One standout appetizer from the 1950s is the burning bush. This simple and comically absurd retro appetizer was a regular go-to in many of my vintage cookbooks, especially when someone was throwing together an atomic-themed party! Often, they'd simply roll cream cheese with chipped beef or pepperoni, but I need more flavor, so I treated mine like the Brooklyn Jewish deli schmears I used to enjoy with some shallots, herbs, and garlic. Feel free to take your own spin!

✦ *Makes 20 to 30 servings*

3 ounces (84 g) cream cheese, softened
1 tablespoon (4 g) finely minced
    fresh parsley
1 teaspoon (5 g) finely minced shallot
1 garlic clove, grated with a Microplane
    grater

½ cup (120 g) finely minced chipped
    beef
Pimento-stuffed olives, for garnish
    (optional)
1 grapefruit or large apple
Lettuce leaves, for serving

1. In a medium bowl, combine the cream cheese, parsley, shallot, and garlic. Mix well and form into bite-size balls by rolling between your hands or shaping with two teaspoons.

2. Put the chipped beef in a shallow bowl. Roll the cream cheese balls around in the chipped beef, ensuring each ball is fully covered.

3. Place a toothpick through each "burning bush," topping off with an olive if using, and anchor the bottom of each toothpick into the grapefruit or apple.

4. Place on top of a bed of lettuce for decoration and serve.

NOTES: *If you'd like to add more to this recipe, get creative! These cream cheese balls would be lovely with finely diced chiles or by folding in more spices, so have fun with this one!*

*A Microplane is a wonderful tool to quickly mince garlic in seconds.*

# FRANK 'N' POTATO PIE

◇◇◇◇◇◇◇◇◇◇◇◇◇◇◇◇◇◇◇◇◇◇◇◇  **1950s**  ◇◇◇◇◇◇◇◇◇◇◇◇◇◇◇◇◇◇◇◇◇◇◇◇

**MEALS** like this were quite popular during the 1950s and '60s. It was a time when hot dogs were having a moment, and would often be served in almost any way you can imagine—even encased in gelatin. We'll skip that recipe this time and lean into something you should actually make.

Give this kitschy but flavorful treat a try the next time you're planning a summer get-together. It's perfect for packing up, easy to reheat, and will be the talk of the table.  ✦ *Makes 4 servings*

| | |
|---|---|
| 8 hot dogs (1 pound) | 1 cup (120 g) shredded sharp cheddar |
| 2 russet potatoes, peeled and diced | cheese, plus more for garnish |
| Salt and ground black pepper to taste | ¼ cup (12 g) finely chopped fresh chives, |
| 1 cup (235 mL) heavy cream | plus more for garnish |
| 5 fresh thyme sprigs | 1 tablespoon hot sauce |
| 1 fresh rosemary branch | ½ teaspoon ground mustard |
| 3 garlic cloves, gently crushed | 1 tablespoon olive oil |

1. Cut six of the hot dogs in half crosswise. Finely chop the remaining two hot dogs.

2. Place the potatoes in a pot of cold water, add a generous pinch of salt, partially cover, and bring to a boil. Cook until fork-tender, 10 to 15 minutes. Drain.

3. While the potatoes are cooking, add the cream, thyme, rosemary, and garlic to a small saucepan and bring to a simmer over medium heat; simmer for 10 minutes.

4. Pass the potatoes through a potato ricer or press through a mesh strainer. Do not use a blender or food processor, as this will make the potatoes gummy rather than pillowy. Return the milled potatoes to the pot and cook over medium-low heat for several minutes. When a skin of potato starch begins to form around the base of the pot, strain half of the hot cream mixture into the potatoes and mix with a spoon or spatula. Add more of the hot cream until you have the consistency you'd like; you may not need it all. Stir in the cheese, chives, hot sauce, and mustard and remove from the heat.

5. In a small sauté pan, add the oil and sauté the chopped hot dogs over medium heat until they have a little color on them, 8 to 10 minutes. Once finished, fold them into the potato mixture. Add the hot dog "spears" to the pan and sauté until they have a bit of color too, 5 to 10 minutes.

6. Transfer the potatoes to a serving bowl, then fence in the potatoes with the hotdog halves. Garnish with chives and more cheese and season with black pepper. Serve.

# PEANUT BUTTER SOUP

THIS recipe continues to surprise me because it always exceeds my expectations. I thought it sounded unappetizing, so I was amazed by how delicious it turned out. The dish has a subtle complexity from the bay leaf and the peanut butter, resulting in a rich and intriguing soup rather than a thick, sweet mess. I would gladly enjoy it at any dinner!

This particular dish was originally brought to America during the transatlantic slave trade, originating from the West African *maafe*, or peanut stew. After the Civil War, the popularity of the soup began to grow, especially in the Southern states, and was even considered a delicacy that would be served at house parties. During the 1950s, with the growing availability of ingredients, the interest for Americans to try "new foods" was at an all-time high. The popularity of Peanut Butter Soup reflects the increasing adventurousness of American cooks. ✦ *Makes 4 servings*

2 tablespoons (28 g) unsalted butter
2 tablespoons (16 g) all-purpose flour
1 onion, minced
4 cups (960 mL) whole milk, cold
1 bay leaf

⅛ teaspoon (0.25 g) freshly grated nutmeg
½ cup (125 g) smooth peanut butter
Salt and ground black pepper to taste
Chopped fresh thyme leaves, for garnish
Oyster crackers, for serving

1. In a large pot, melt the butter over medium-low heat. Add the flour and onion and cook, stirring frequently, for 5 minutes. Add the cold milk, turn the heat up to medium-high, and cook, whisking until the mixture begins to thicken slightly.

2. Add the bay leaf, nutmeg, and peanut butter and season to taste with salt and pepper, whisking until smooth.

3. Turn the heat back down to medium-low and allow the soup to simmer for 30 minutes to extract maximum flavor from the bay leaf.

4. Remove the bay leaf. Working in batches as necessary, transfer the soup to a blender (or use an immersion blender) and puree until smooth.

5. Garnish with chopped thyme and serve with oyster crackers.

# DR PEPPER BEAN DIP

◇◇◇◇◇◇◇◇◇◇◇◇◇◇◇◇◇◇◇◇◇◇◇  **1960s**  ◇◇◇◇◇◇◇◇◇◇◇◇◇◇◇◇◇◇◇◇◇◇◇

T H I S unusual recipe name might make you hesitate, but I promise this dish is not just delicious—it will also leave you curious about what other colas you could use in cooking! Throughout the twentieth century, food companies would often create recipe books to be included with products or received upon submission of certain proofs of purchase. Cola companies caught on to this trend, creating small brochures with a few creative recipes, encouraging their buyers to buy even more of their products so they could try out the recipes. The surprising thing is that cooking with cola is delicious!

I originally discovered this recipe in a fun little book titled *Cookin' with Dr Pepper*, published in the mid-1960s. I don't think there's a single dish in there that isn't great! ✦ *Makes about 2 cups*

1 (15.5 oz/439 g) can cannellini beans, rinsed and drained

1 (4-ounce/113 g) can chopped green chiles, drained

½ cup (120 mL) Dr Pepper

2 tablespoons (45 g) tomato paste

2 tablespoons (30 mL) olive oil

2 garlic cloves, minced

1½ teaspoons (8 mL) Worcestershire sauce

1 teaspoon (5 g) salt

1 cup (113 g) shredded sharp cheddar cheese

½ cup (115 g) crispy bacon crumbles

½ cup (25 g) finely chopped fresh chives

Potato chips or Canapé Crackers (page 70), for serving

1. In a large pot, combine the beans, chiles, Dr Pepper, tomato paste, olive oil, garlic, Worcestershire sauce, and salt. Bring to a boil over medium-high heat and cook, stirring occasionally, for 3 to 5 minutes, until fragrant and thickened.

2. Working in batches as necessary, transfer the bean mixture to a blender, add the shredded cheese, and blend on high into a smooth paste. Or use an immersion blender to puree the mixture in the pot.

3. Pass the dip through a fine-mesh strainer to remove anything that did not get pureed.

4. Pour the dip into a bowl, top with the crispy bacon and chives, and serve warm or at room temperature with your favorite chips or crackers.

**N O T E S :** *This dip can be made with different beans, like great northern or black beans.*

# The ORIGINAL CAESAR SALAD

THE Caesar salad, still one of the most beloved dishes on menus today, was created somewhat by accident. In 1924, Caesar Cardini, an Italian immigrant and chef living in Tijuana, Mexico, found himself overwhelmed with orders from American tourists celebrating the Fourth of July. Faced with limited ingredients in his kitchen, he combined mashed anchovies, egg yolk, lime juice, and Parmesan cheese to create the dressing and tossed it with romaine lettuce. As the saying goes, the rest is history! ✦ *Makes 6 servings*

6 anchovy fillets, drained and chopped
1 teaspoon (5 g) Dijon mustard
1 garlic clove, minced
2 large egg yolks
Juice of 1 lime
1 teaspoon (5 mL) Worcestershire sauce
¾ cup (180 mL) extra-virgin olive oil

¼ cup (22 g) grated Parmesan cheese, plus more for serving
Kosher salt and ground black pepper to taste
3 romaine hearts, leaves separated but left whole
Croutons, for serving

1. In a food processor, process the anchovies, mustard, garlic, egg yolks, lime juice, and Worcestershire sauce until smooth. (Alternatively, you can use a large mortar and pestle.) Transfer to a medium bowl.

2. Gradually add the olive oil, drop by drop, while whisking rapidly and progressively adding more oil until the dressing begins to emulsify.

3. Add the Parmesan cheese and season with salt and pepper to taste.

4. Put the lettuce leaves in a large bowl. Spoon a couple tablespoons of the dressing on the lettuce and toss to incorporate.

5. Plate the salads and top with more Parmesan cheese and croutons. Serve right away.

**NOTE:** *There shouldn't be any concern with the raw egg yolks, as the acid from the lime juice is enough to kill any potential bacteria, but if you'd like to take additional precautions, you can boil the eggs briefly, which will pasteurize them. Simply add the eggs to a pot of boiling water and boil for about 1 minute, then transfer to a bowl of ice water to cool completely. Crack the eggs open and discard the egg whites.*

# RED DEVIL

THIS dish—a kind of cousin of Welsh rarebit—was known to be one of Bing Crosby's favorites. According to *What Actors Eat When They Eat!* from 1939, he was quoted as saying, "The combination of ingredients in this dish gives it a rare flavor, which is particularly tempting when one's appetite needs a 'lift.'"

I can confirm that this seemingly simple meal is definitely worth reviving, especially since making the tomato soup from scratch enhances the flavors. However, if you're short on time, a can of good-quality tomato soup will work just fine.  ✦ *Makes 4 servings*

| | |
|---|---|
| 1 (10-ounce/283 g) can crushed tomatoes | Salt and ground black pepper to taste |
| ½ onion, finely diced | 1 tablespoon (15 mL) olive oil |
| 6 garlic cloves, finely minced | 2 cups (300 g) frozen peas |
| 4 or 5 large basil leaves | 1 pound (450 g) cheddar cheese, shredded |
| 1 bay leaf | 2 large eggs |
| 1 teaspoon (5 g) sugar | 8 slices bread, toasted |

1. In a large pot, combine the tomatoes, onion, 5 of the minced garlic cloves, the basil, bay leaf, sugar, and salt. Bring to a simmer over medium heat and simmer gently for 15 to 20 minutes, until reduced by one quarter. Taste for seasoning and balance as needed with salt and pepper. Discard the whole herbs and puree the soup with an immersion blender until it is as smooth as you like. (Alternatively, you can strain the soup through a sieve.)

2. In a sauté pan, heat the oil over medium-low heat. Add the remaining minced garlic and cook until fragrant but not browning, about 5 minutes. Pour the contents of the pan into the pot with the strained soup. Add the frozen peas and the cheese and simmer over medium-low heat for several minutes to warm the peas and melt the cheese.

3. In a small bowl, beat the eggs with a fork or whisk until frothy. Remove the pot from the heat and fold the beaten eggs into the tomato soup, whisking constantly to prevent the eggs from scrambling.

4. Immediately serve, while warm, over freshly toasted bread.

NOTE: *I know from years of sharing these recipes online that many people dislike peas, which is a shame, since they offer a wonderful taste and surprising "pop" in this dish. But, if you're partial to pushing away the peas, you can absolutely substitute another tasty treat, like roasted and chopped broccoli or even beans or legumes to give your red devil a bit more substance.*

# BAKED CARROT RING with PEAS

FOOD from the mid-century always brings a smile to my face. Each dish feels like it serves a distinct purpose in its design. Similar to the Burning Bush (page 35) or any aspic in this book, many of the recipes were simply strung together to be a little odd—and a lot more fun to look at after Happy Hour. That's why I fell in love with this recipe; it's not only delicious but also incredibly fun to make and enjoy!

I wanted to elevate this dish by including a bit more technique and utilizing fresh ingredients, rather than canned cream-of-something soup, canned peas, and a pinch of despair.

✦ *Makes 6 servings*

**FOR THE SOUFFLÉ BASE**
4 large eggs, separated
2 tablespoons (28 g) unsalted butter
1 shallot, minced
2 garlic cloves, finely minced
Salt to taste
¼ cup (32 g) all-purpose flour
1 cup (240 mL) whole milk
2 cups (480 g) pureed carrots

**FOR THE SAUCE SUPRÊME**
2 tablespoons (28 g) unsalted butter
2 tablespoons (16 g) all-purpose flour
1 cup (240 mL) Homemade Chicken Stock
    (page 225)

½ cup (120 mL) heavy cream
2 tablespoons (about 6 g) fresh thyme
    leaves
Salt and ground black pepper to taste
1 cup (150 g) frozen peas

**FOR SERVING**
Soft fresh herbs (such as parsley, basil,
    cilantro, dill), torn
2 tablespoons (30 mL) extra-virgin
    olive oil
Flaky salt and freshly cracked black
    pepper to taste

1. Preheat the oven to 375°F (190°C). Grease a 4-cup ring mold (or six individual molds).

2. Whip the egg whites to stiff peaks in a bowl or stand mixer. Set aside.

3. In a medium pot, melt the butter over medium-low heat. Add the shallot, garlic, and salt and cook for several minutes, until softened and fragrant. Add the flour and cook for 5 minutes to remove the raw flour taste. Add the milk and whisk until the sauce thickens.

4. Off the heat, add the egg yolks, one at a time, whisking constantly to avoid scrambling them. Then gradually fold in the carrot puree, and then fold in the whipped egg whites.

5. Transfer the soufflé base to the prepared ring mold, then place the mold in a large roasting pan. Pour enough water into the roasting pan to come halfway up the side of the ring mold. Carefully transfer to the oven and bake for 30 minutes, or until set.

6. While the soufflé is baking, prepare the sauce. Melt the butter in a small saucepan over medium heat. Add the flour and cook for several minutes to remove the raw flour taste. Add the chicken stock, cream, and thyme. Whisk and cook until the sauce thickens, then season with salt and pepper to taste. Add the frozen peas and allow to warm through.

7. When the soufflé is finished, turn it out onto a serving platter. Fill the center of the ring with the peas and most of the sauce. Drizzle the remaining sauce on the soufflé, then top the peas with the herbs. Drizzle with the olive oil, season with flaky salt and cracked black pepper, and serve.

# RABBIT RICE MOLD

WELSH rabbit, also known as Welsh rarebit, is a centuries-old dish from the United Kingdom. Despite its name, it does not traditionally contain rabbit; rather, it consists of fancy toast topped with a cheese sauce. This recipe enhances the traditional preparation by using rice instead of toast and incorporates peas, which complement the cheese sauce nicely. ✦ *Makes 6 servings*

1 cup (150 g) frozen peas
4 large eggs, hard-boiled
1 tablespoon (14 g) unsalted butter
1 tablespoon (8 g) all-purpose flour
½ cup (120 mL) milk
½ cup (120 mL) stout beer
1 cup (113 g) shredded sharp cheddar cheese

1 teaspoon (5 g) salt, plus more to taste
Freshly ground black pepper, to taste (optional)
½ teaspoon (2.5 g) ground mustard
½ teaspoon (2.5 mL) Worcestershire sauce
1 cup (200 g) white rice, freshly cooked
Chopped fresh parsley, for garnish

1. Bring a small saucepan of salted water to a boil. Add the frozen peas and blanch for 30 seconds, then immediately remove the peas with a strainer and transfer them to a large bowl of ice water. This will stop the cooking process and make the peas more vibrantly green. Once cooled, drain and set aside.

2. Peel the hard-boiled eggs and slice each in half. Season the cut sides with a pinch of salt and a few grinds of pepper, if using. Set aside.

3. In a small saucepan, melt the butter over medium-low heat. Whisk in the flour and cook for several minutes, until nutty and fragrant. Add the milk and beer and whisk until the sauce begins to thicken. Add the shredded cheese and season with the salt, mustard, and Worcestershire sauce. Cook until the cheese is melted, then remove from the heat.

4. Grease a 4-cup ring mold. Spoon the hot cooked rice into the ring mold and allow it to sit for 5 minutes to set, then invert it onto a serving platter. Fill the center of the ring with the blanched peas. Pour the cheese sauce over everything. Arrange the egg halves on the outside of the rice ring and garnish with parsley on top. Serve immediately.

# BEET SALAD

THIS particular dish may seem silly, but it makes more sense than many other aspic recipes I've tried over the years. It's also more appealing to the general public than the poached egg in aspic that I made from Julia Child's recipe—no thanks to that one!

This dish is filled with wonderful, earthy flavors that pair nicely with the lightly sweetened flavored gelatin. It works particularly well in smaller, individual molds. While you can definitely use another flavor of gelatin, I believe that lemon-lime works best. ✦ *Makes 6 servings*

1 (3-ounce/85 g) package lemon-lime–flavored gelatin
¾ teaspoon (4 g) salt
1 cup (240 mL) boiling water
¾ cup (180 mL) pomegranate juice

1 teaspoon (5 g) prepared horseradish
2 teaspoons (6 g) finely diced shallot
¾ cup (100 g) finely diced cooked beets
¾ cup (100 g) finely diced celery

1. In a medium heatproof bowl, stir the gelatin and salt into the boiling water until they dissolve. Add the pomegranate juice and horseradish, stir well, and refrigerate until very thick but not quite set, about 1 hour.

2. Fold the shallot, beets, and celery into the gelatin.

3. Grease a 4 cup (1 L) mold (or six individual molds). Spoon the gelatin mixture into the mold and chill until firm, 2 to 3 hours.

4. When ready to unmold, place a hot, wet kitchen towel over the outside of the mold. The heat should loosen the gelatin slightly. Gently shake the mold to break the vacuum inside, then serve immediately.

NOTE: *If your mold does not come out clean, just return the gelatin mixture to the mold and allow it to reset in the refrigerator. You can also wrap a hot, wet towel around the mold to loosen it. Or next time try adding a light coating of nonstick spray to the inside of the mold before filling. Even if it doesn't look great, it will be ugly delicious!*

# SUNSET SALAD

◇◇◇◇◇◇◇◇◇◇◇◇◇◇◇◇◇◇◇◇◇◇◇◇  **1960s**  ◇◇◇◇◇◇◇◇◇◇◇◇◇◇◇◇◇◇◇◇◇◇◇◇

ONE of the most common questions I get from folks regarding any dish that includes gelatin is "But did it taste good?" Usually the answer is "Absolutely not." Therefore, I made sure to include some gelatin recipes in this book that I *genuinely* enjoy and believe are worth making.

I found this recipe in the *Joys of Jell-O* cookbook and, after trying it, knew this was absolutely worth repeating, as this particular dish is truly delightful. It's the perfect representation of a mid-century "salad," since pineapple was often included in recipes as a status ingredient—they weren't cheap or easy to come by! Garnish with some lettuce at its base and it checks all the boxes for taste and texture. ✦ *Makes 6 servings*

1 (3-ounce/85 g) package lemon- or
  orange-flavored gelatin
½ teaspoon (3 g) salt
1½ cups (360 mL) boiling water
1 (8-ounce/227 g) can crushed
  pineapple, undrained

1 tablespoon (15 mL) lemon juice
1 cup (100 g) grated carrots, plus more
  for garnish
½ cup (60 g) chopped walnuts
Lettuce leaves, for garnish

1. In a medium heatproof bowl, stir the gelatin and salt into the boiling water until they dissolve. Whisk in the pineapple and lemon juice. Refrigerate for 1 hour, or until it begins to thicken.

2. Grease a 3-cup (710 ml) mold (or six individual molds). Fold the carrots and walnuts into the gelatin and transfer the mixture to the prepared mold. Refrigerate for 2 to 3 hours or until completely firm.

3. Warm the exterior of the mold by dipping it into a large pot of warm water, then unmold it onto a plate covered with a bed of lettuce. Garnish with grated carrot and serve.

# POTATO and ONION PIEROGI

PIEROGI are, in my humble opinion, perhaps the perfect food. They consist of a delightful pasta-like shell filled with creamy mashed potatoes, onions, and cheese, which is boiled and then pan-fried. Served with applesauce and sour cream, they make my mouth water just thinking about them. Traditionally, pierogi are savory, but they can also be spicy, sweet, or salty, with a variety of fillings, including cabbage, sausage, or even fruits.

Pierogi's history in American culture traces back to the early 1900s. During that time, Polish immigrants came to the United States seeking a fresh start and quickly introduced Poland's national dish to the Americans within their communities. However, it wasn't until after World War II that pierogi became popular for fundraisers, gaining more recognition among non-Polish community members. By the 1960s, pierogi were commonly found in the freezer aisle of almost every grocery store across North America.

Over the years, various companies have put their own spin on these dumplings, but I still hold a special place in my heart for the traditional potato and onion pierogi. My favorite way to serve them is with a bit of applesauce and kielbasa. I consider this one of my "desert island meals"!

✦ *Makes 6 servings*

### FOR THE DOUGH
2 cups (240 g) all-purpose flour, plus
    more if needed
1½ cups (180 g) bread flour
1 large egg, beaten
2 teaspoons (10 g) salt
½ cup (120 mL) water

### FOR THE FILLING
1 to 2 tablespoons olive oil
2 white onions, finely diced
3 large garlic cloves, finely diced
2 russet potatoes, peeled and diced
½ cup (120 mL) heavy cream

2 tablespoons (about 6 g) fresh thyme
    leaves, chopped
2 teaspoons (10 g) salt

### FOR FRYING
2 to 4 tablespoons unsalted butter

### FOR SERVING
3 tablespoons (42 g) unsalted butter
½ cup (25 g) panko breadcrumbs
Chopped fresh parsley
Grated Parmesan cheese
Applesauce
Sour cream
Cooked kielbasa

*Recipe continues* ➤

1. In a stand mixer fitted with the paddle attachment, combine the all-purpose flour, bread flour, egg, and salt and mix on medium-low speed, gradually adding the water until a ball of dough begins to form. Switch to the dough hook attachment and knead for about 10 minutes on medium-low speed. If the dough is very wet, add a tablespoon of flour at a time until the dough is shiny and not tacky to the touch. Turn the dough out into a lightly oiled bowl and cover with a damp towel or plastic wrap to rest for about 30 minutes.

2. While the dough is resting, make the filling. In a medium sauté pan, add the olive oil, onions, garlic, a pinch of salt, and 1 cup of water. Bring to a boil and cover, allowing to cook for 8 to 10 minutes while the liquid slowly evaporates.

3. When the liquid has evaporated from the pan, the onions will quickly begin to brown. Lower the heat to medium and continue to move the onions until they gradually take on more color, deglazing the fond on the pan with a few tablespoons of water, stock, or even white wine. After about 20 minutes, they will be golden brown, soft, and sweet. Set aside.

4. Bring a medium pot of water to a boil. Add the potatoes and cook until fork-tender. Drain, then pass the potatoes through a ricer. Do not use a food processor or blender since that will make them gluey. Return the potatoes to the pot and add the caramelized onions and garlic, cream, thyme, and salt. Mix well.

5. Roll the dough out on a lightly floured surface until it's about $\frac{1}{8}$ inch thick. Using a 3-inch circular ring mold, cut out the pierogi wrappers. Fill each wrapper with a generous tablespoon of the potato and onion filling. Fold the dough over to make a half-moon shape, crimp the edges, and cover with a damp towel to keep from drying out.

6. Bring a large pot of salted water to a boil. Working in batches, drop the pierogi in and cook for 5 minutes. Using a slotted spoon, transfer to a plate.

7. To pan-fry the pierogi, melt the butter in a large skillet over medium heat. Working in batches, fry the pierogi until they're crispy and golden, 4 to 5 minutes on each side. Transfer to a plate.

8. To toast the breadcrumbs, melt the butter in the same pan over medium heat. Add the breadcrumbs and cook until toasted but not burnt, 3 to 4 minutes.

9. Top the pierogi with the toasted breadcrumbs, some fresh parsley, and Parmesan cheese. Serve with a spoonful of applesauce, sour cream, and kielbasa.

# TOMATO ASPIC

◇◇◇◇◇◇◇◇◇◇◇◇◇◇◇◇◇◇◇◇◇◇  **1950s**  ◇◇◇◇◇◇◇◇◇◇◇◇◇◇◇◇◇◇◇◇◇◇

ONE of the most recognizable mid-century recipes is undoubtedly aspic, a type of gelatin dish. An aspic is essentially a savory jelly made from slowly rendered meat stock, which is rich in collagen. When this collagen breaks down, it transforms into gelatin. This technique has been used for centuries, with some of the earliest printed mentions dating back to around the year 1300.

Typically, these dishes served more as a lavish centerpiece for admiration than as something you would actually eat. However, I find that tomato aspic is quite enjoyable! I've experimented with many recipes, but I particularly love this version, which includes horseradish for a peppery kick that really awakens the palate. Not only will it be a stunning salad to share with friends, but it also offers a delightful retro taste! ✦ *Makes 8 servings*

2 tablespoons (about 20 g) unflavored gelatin
½ cup (120 mL) cold water
4 cups (1 L) tomato juice
2 tablespoons (30 mL) lemon juice
1 teaspoon (5 mL) Worcestershire sauce
1 tablespoon (15 g) prepared horseradish
2 tablespoons (about 20 g) finely diced cucumber
2 tablespoons (about 20 g) finely minced onion

1 garlic clove, finely minced
1 teaspoon (5 g) sugar
1 tablespoon (10 g) salt
1 Bouquet Garni (page 229)

FOR SERVING
Fresh curly parsley sprigs
Cucumber wheels
Crostini or toast points

1. In a small bowl, stir the gelatin into the water and allow to bloom for 5 to 10 minutes.

2. In a large pot, combine the tomato juice, lemon juice, Worcestershire sauce, horseradish, cucumber, onion, garlic, sugar, and salt and bring to a boil. Immediately turn the heat down to medium-low. Add the bouquet garni and bloomed gelatin and simmer for 15 minutes, stirring occasionally.

3. Lightly coat the inside of a 4- to 6-cup (1–1.5 L) mold (see Note) with butter or nonstick spray. Pour the warm tomato liquid into the mold. Refrigerate until fully set, at least 5 hours.

4. When ready to serve, invert the mold onto a serving plate and place a hot, wet towel on top of the mold to help release the aspic. Garnish with parsley and cucumber wheels and serve with crostini or toast points.

NOTE: *If you use a ring-style mold, you can load the center of the tomato aspic with a delicious filling of shrimp salad, crudité, or anything else your heart desires!*

# BREADS & SANDWICHES

**FOR** nearly fourteen thousand years, bread has been an integral part of our culinary history. It has long been regarded as the Great Unifier. When we welcome someone into our home or take a client out to dinner, we often use the expression "breaking bread" to suggest connection and hospitality. Dips, oils, and spreads have been created to enhance a simple loaf or flatbread, keeping it a communal tradition to share and enjoy with friends, family, and even strangers.

Many of the world's most delicious breads are made with indigenous ingredients, resulting in unique variations across cultures. From the types of grains used to the local water sources, and whether a leavening agent is included or if a sourdough starter is created from scratch, there are easily over one hundred distinctly different types of bread, each of which offers its own particular characteristics.

The recipes in this chapter have been selected for their uniqueness and deliciousness, representing a century of culinary evolution. You'll discover depth and variety in flavors and textures, as well as recipes that may change the way you approach baking bread.

The story goes that it wasn't until the mid-1700s that the fourth Earl of Sandwich, a gambler, requested roasted beef to be placed between two slices of bread so he wouldn't have to interrupt his card games to eat. While the accuracy of this tale is debated, there may be some truth to it. It's a time-saver for sure!

From open-faced to dressed, fried, and even stuffed varieties, *Retro Recipes* showcases some of the most unique and delicious sandwiches I have encountered during my culinary journey. There are, of course, many more sandwiches to discover, so if you want to dive deeper into the wonderful world of sandwiches, I recommend my friend Barry Enderwick's book, *Sandwiches of History*.

My hope is that you not only try each of these unique breads and sandwiches, but that you add your own flair to them! Let's keep the human tradition of breaking bread alive.

# ANADAMA BREAD

NEW England has provided us with centuries of incredible recipes that have stood the test of time, such as whoopie pies, baked beans, and clam chowder. One of my favorite New England dishes, though less celebrated, is the delicious anadama bread.

Although a recipe for anadama bread was first printed in the 1910s, this bread was likely made in colonial homes long before then. The story goes that Anna, who was not a great cook, tried to feed her temperamental husband a sweet gruel made from cornmeal and molasses. In frustration, he shouted, "Anna, damn her!" and threw flour into the mixture before baking it to salvage the mess. The result was a delicious bread, and the name has stuck, influenced by the thick New England accent. Serve it toasted, topped with your favorite preserves, jam, or sweet butter. ✦ *Makes 2 loaves*

1 (¼-ounce/7 g) packet active dry yeast
2½ cups (600 mL) warm water
½ cup (60 g) cornmeal
3 tablespoons (42 g) unsalted butter, softened, plus 2 tablespoons melted butter for glazing

½ cup (130 g) molasses
1 teaspoon (5 g) salt
1 teaspoon (5 g) sugar
5 cups (600 g) all-purpose flour, sifted
Flaky sea salt, for sprinkling

1. In a small bowl, add the yeast to $1/2$ cup of the warm water and set aside. In another small bowl, add the cornmeal to another 1 cup water. Bring the remaining 1 cup water to a boil in a small saucepan. Add the cornmeal mixture to the boiling water, turn the heat down to medium-low, and cook for about 6 minutes, or until the mixture thickens. Remove from the heat, add the butter, molasses, salt, and sugar, and mix to incorporate. Set aside to cool until warm, below 120°F (48°C).

2. In a stand mixer or by hand, add the yeast mixture to the cooled cornmeal mixture. Stir in the flour, 1 cup at a time, and blend until a dough begins to form.

3. Knead for about 10 minutes, or until the dough relaxes a bit and develops a smooth surface. Place the dough in a large, oiled bowl, cover with a towel, and set aside in a warm environment until it doubles in size, 1 to 2 hours.

4. Grease two 9 × 4-inch loaf pans. Turn the dough out onto a lightly floured surface. Punch down the dough and divide it in half. For each loaf, fold the top, bottom, and sides into itself and place inside the greased bread pan. Set aside to proof, covered with a damp towel, for another 40 minutes. Meanwhile, preheat the oven to 350°F (175°C) with a rack in the middle position.

5. Bake for about 45 minutes, or until the loaf is golden brown on top and makes a hollow sound when you tap the bottom. While the loaves are still warm, glaze with melted butter and sprinkle with flaky sea salt. Cool on a rack before cutting and serving.

# BOSTON BROWN BREAD

1920s

ONE of New England's lesser-known creations comes from Boston, where the distinctive steamed bread known as Boston brown bread—or "bread in a can"—was invented. Still produced by the B&M brand, it can be found today in many grocery stores, usually located in the flour aisle. What makes this bread unique is that it does not use yeast, unlike many traditional breads, and is prepared using a steaming process, often in an old-fashioned coffee can.

Traditionally, bakers would include buttermilk, a tangy by-product of soured milk, along with baking soda to react with the natural acidity of the buttermilk. Although the bread requires about 3 hours of steaming to achieve its perfect texture, the result is a flavorful, subtly sweet, and slightly tangy loaf that is well worth the wait. ✦ *Makes 1 large or 2 smaller loaves*

1 cup (120 g) all-purpose flour, sifted

1 cup (120 g) whole wheat or rye flour, sifted

1 cup (120 g) cornmeal

2 teaspoons (6 g) baking soda

2 teaspoons (10 g) salt

¾ cup (160 g) molasses

2 cups (475 mL) buttermilk

1 cup (145 g) raisins, dusted lightly with flour (optional)

1. Combine the all-purpose flour, whole wheat flour, cornmeal, baking soda, and salt in a large bowl and mix well.

2. In a small bowl, combine the molasses and buttermilk. Add the mixture to the dry ingredients and mix until a batter forms. Add the raisins (if using).

3. Line the bottom of an 8-cup (2 L) mold, or two clean, empty coffee cans, with parchment paper and generously grease the parchment and sides with nonstick spray. Fill the prepared mold or cans two-thirds of the way with batter and cover with aluminum foil. Tie the foil tightly with butcher's twine or a thick rubber band.

4. Place a trivet in a Dutch oven or other large pot. Place the mold or cans on the trivet. Fill the Dutch oven with enough water to come halfway up the mold or cans and allow the water to come to a rolling boil over high heat.

5. Cover the Dutch oven and cook for about 3 hours, occasionally adding water to the Dutch oven to ensure it's not dry. When done, the center of the bread should read about 200°F (94°C) on an instant-read thermometer.

6. Allow the bread to cool inside the mold or can for 10 minutes. Remove the foil, invert the mold or can, and unmold by tapping the bottom with your palm or opening the bottom of the can and pressing through the other side. Cool completely before serving.

# MILK TOAST

MANY recipes from the past were born out of necessity, scarcity, and genuine creativity. One such recipe that stands out for me is milk toast. Originally, this dish was considered a mild meal suitable for the sick and often appeared in cookbook sections labeled "Invalid Cookery." However, this does not diminish its appeal; milk toast is delicious, inexpensive, and incredibly simple to prepare!

Traditionally, milk toast involves toasting bread and pouring sweetened hot milk over it. In contrast, the method I'm sharing achieves a similar result but with a custardy texture by cooking the ingredients in a pan and gradually adding the sweetened milk. It's truly delightful when served with fresh berries. ✦ *Makes 2 servings*

| | |
|---|---|
| 4 slices bread, preferably stale | ¼ cup (60 mL) milk |
| 4 tablespoons (56 g) unsalted butter, softened | 2 tablespoons (30 mL) sweetened condensed milk |
| 1 teaspoon (5 g) sugar | Fresh fruit, for serving (optional) |

1. Butter the bread on both sides and sprinkle with the sugar. Make two stacks of two slices of bread.

2. Heat a large sauté pan over medium heat. Place the bread stacks in the pan, side by side. Pour half of the milk on top of the bread and allow the heat to crisp the bread while it absorbs the milk, 3 to 4 minutes.

3. When the bread is beginning to brown, flip it over with a spatula and pour the remaining milk on top. Cook until the bread is browned on the other side, then transfer to a cutting board. Cut the bread into small cubes. Place the cubes in a bowl and drizzle the sweetened condensed milk on top.

4. Serve as is or with fresh fruit for a light, sweet, and delicious breakfast that will keep you running for hours.

# BUTTERMILK BREAD

◇◇◇◇◇◇◇◇◇◇◇◇◇◇◇ **1860s** ◇◇◇◇◇◇◇◇◇◇◇◇◇◇◇

ONE of the key principles of our ancestral cooking was the importance of minimizing waste during meal preparation. Vegetable scraps and meat trimmings were often used to create flavorful stocks, while leftover mashed potatoes could be transformed into croquettes the next day. Every meal was thoughtfully planned to ensure that little was discarded. Naturally, buttermilk, which is a fermented by-product of churning butter, found its way into our baking. It adds a refreshingly bright flavor and has the ideal chemistry for creating light, tangy beverages and baked goods.

This buttermilk bread is exceptionally soft, with a subtle zing, making it perfect for sandwiches or for use in The Frosted Sandwich Loaf (page 78). ✦ *Makes 2 loaves*

| | |
|---|---|
| 1 cup (240 mL) buttermilk | 1 (¼-ounce/7 g) packet active dry yeast |
| 3 tablespoons (42 g) sugar | 1 cup (240 mL) warm water |
| 2½ teaspoons (12 g) salt | ¼ teaspoon (2 g) baking powder |
| ⅓ cup (75 g) unsalted butter, plus 2 tablespoons melted butter for glazing | 6 cups (720 g) all-purpose flour, sifted |
| | Flaky sea salt, for sprinkling |

1. Scald the buttermilk in a small saucepan over medium heat until it begins to curdle, then stir in the sugar, salt, and butter. Set aside to cool until warm, below 120°F (48°C).

2. In a large bowl, add the yeast to the warm water and allow to bloom for 10 minutes.

3. Stir the buttermilk mixture into the yeast mixture, then add the baking powder. Stir in the flour, 1 cup at a time, until you have a dough with a rough, dull appearance. It will be mildly tacky.

4. Turn the dough out onto a lightly floured surface and knead until smooth, about 10 minutes. Transfer the dough to a greased bowl and set aside to rest until doubled in size, about 1 hour.

5. Grease two 9 × 5-inch loaf pans. Turn the dough back out onto the counter and punch out the air, then divide it in half. Transfer the dough to the prepared pans, cover with a towel, and allow to proof for 30 to 40 minutes, or until the dough springs back in about 5 seconds when you press a finger into it. Meanwhile, preheat the oven to 375°F (190°C) with a rack in the middle position.

6. Uncover the loaves and bake for about 35 minutes, or until they are golden brown on top and make a hollow sound when you tap the bottom.

7. While the loaves are still warm, glaze with melted butter and sprinkle with flaky sea salt. Cool completely on a wire rack before slicing and serving.

# COPYCAT CHEEZ-IT CRACKERS

1930s

WITHOUT hesitation, I can say that one of my favorite snacks in the world is Cheez-It crackers. They're crispy, savory, and just a handful (or eleven) usually satisfies my appetite. When I came across a brilliant copycat recipe in *The Party Cookbook* from 1954, I knew I had to try it, and it did not disappoint. While the texture is a bit different from commercial Cheez-It crackers, the flavor is even better and is sure to impress your guests!

You can also enjoy these sandwiched with homemade Pimento Cheese (page 72) for an easy and fun canapé. ✦ *Makes about 250 crackers*

1 cup (100 g) walnuts or pecans
1 cup (225 g) unsalted butter, softened
8 ounces (225 g) yellow cheddar cheese, freshly shredded

2½ cups (300 g) all-purpose flour
2½ teaspoons (12 g) salt
1 teaspoon (3 g) sweet paprika
Kosher salt, for dusting

1. Add the walnuts or pecans to a food processor and pulse briefly until they are finely ground. Avoid overprocessing into a puree. Remove the ground nuts to a bowl and set aside.

2. Cream together the butter and cheddar in the food processor until they come together into a paste. Add the ground nuts, flour, salt, and paprika and pulse several times until a dough forms. Wrap the dough in plastic wrap and refrigerate for 1 hour. This will allow the dough to hydrate and the butter to cool again before rolling.

3. Divide the dough into four equal portions. Lightly dust with flour and roll each portion between two sheets of parchment paper to a thickness of a quarter. Using a sharp knife or rolling cutter, score the dough vertically and horizontally to make a grid of 1-inch crackers. Then use a dowel or chopstick to make an indentation in the center of each cracker. Allow to rest for 30 minutes.

4. Preheat the oven to 350°F (175°C) with a rack in the middle position. Line two rimmed baking sheets with parchment paper or silicone baking mats. Transfer the crackers to the prepared baking sheets, leaving ½ inch between each cracker. Dust the tops of the crackers with kosher salt.

5. Bake in batches for about 15 minutes each in a convection oven or about 20 minutes in a conventional oven, rotating the sheets halfway through to ensure even baking.

6. Allow the crackers to cool on the baking sheet for 5 to 10 minutes, then transfer to your favorite snack bowl and dig in!

**NOTE:** *This recipe works wonderfully with a blend of cheeses. Avoid using preshredded cheese, which often has added cornstarch—you want to grate it yourself from a block.*

# GOUGÈRES (CHEESE PUFFS)

THERE are few things I love making more than choux (pronounced "shoe") pastry. It has unfairly gained a reputation for being too difficult for home cooks to tackle, but it's actually quite simple to prepare. Mastering this one dough opens the door to a variety of delicious dishes, such as these airy, crispy, and cheesy puffs. I owe my obsession with choux pastry to Julia Child, who introduced me to the wonderful world of French cooking. In the 1960s, gougères experienced a spike in popularity as Julia brought a French Wave to the US, along with escargot, baguettes, and my favorite, Boeuf Bourguignon (page 102). Gougères are perfect for your next retro gathering!

✦ *Makes about 2 dozen gougères*

1 cup (240 mL) water
6 tablespoons (84 g) unsalted butter
1 cup (120 g) all-purpose flour
¾ teaspoon (4 g) salt

4 large eggs plus 1 large egg yolk
2 cups (200 g) shredded Gruyère or mild
   cheddar cheese

1. Preheat the oven to 425°F (220°C) with a rack in the middle position. Grease two rimmed baking sheets.

2. In a small saucepan, heat the water and butter over medium heat until the butter is melted. Add the flour and salt and cook, stirring with a spatula, until a dough forms and a skin begins to appear on the bottom of the pot. Remove from the heat and allow to cool for a couple minutes.

3. Add the whole eggs, one at a time, whisking until fully incorporated. The batter will appear to be broken, but keep working at it before adding the next egg. When it's mixed enough, you should be able to spoon some of the batter and have it take roughly 4 seconds to fall back into the bowl. Add the cheese and mix well, then remove from the heat.

4. Spoon (or pipe) the puffs onto the prepared baking sheets in 2-inch discs, leaving 2 to 3 inches between. Beat the egg yolk to make an egg wash, then brush the tops of the puffs. Bake for about 25 minutes, or until the puffs are golden brown. Allow to cool for about 15 minutes and they'll crisp up even more; serve warm.

NOTE: *Once completely cooled, you can store the gougères in an airtight container at room temperature for up to 2 days, or refrigerate for up to 5 days. Warm them back up in a 350°F (175°C) oven for 5 to 10 minutes before serving.*

# PARKER HOUSE ROLLS

COOKING is communal, and the Parker House roll is perhaps one of my favorite tearable treats—not to be confused with The Beef Fizz (page 162), which is simply terrible. These little guys have been a staple of American dining since the 1870s, and were in fact considered to be a happy accident, much like the discovery of penicillin, Teflon, and even the microwave! Legend has it that an angry pastry chef threw his rolls against a wall, resulting in a fold that became a distinctive feature of Parker House rolls. This recipe will have you rushing to make more of these delightful pull-apart rolls in no time! Though perhaps not as impressive as penicillin, these are way more enjoyable. ✦ *Makes 14 rolls*

1 (¼-ounce/7 g) packet active dry yeast

1 cup (240 mL) warm water

4 tablespoons (56 g) unsalted butter, softened, plus 2 tablespoons melted butter for brushing and glazing

1 large egg plus 1 large egg yolk

3 tablespoons (45 g) sugar

1½ teaspoons (8 g) salt

3½ cups (420 g) all-purpose flour, sifted

2 tablespoons (30 g) milk

Flaky sea salt, for sprinkling

1. In a small bowl, add the yeast to the warm water and allow to bloom for 5 to 10 minutes.

2. Combine the softened butter, whole egg, sugar, and salt in a stand mixer fitted with the paddle attachment. (Alternatively, you can do this by hand with a wooden spoon.) Mix on medium-low speed until combined, then add the yeast mixture.

3. Gradually add flour until a dough begins to form. Knead for 5 minutes (or 10 minutes by hand), until the dough is tacky but not sticky. Place the dough in a greased bowl, cover with a towel, and let proof in a warm place for at least 1½ hours, or overnight in the refrigerator for the best result.

4. Punch down the dough and divide into 14 equal portions (about 60 grams each). For the classic Parker House roll shape, roll each portion on a lightly floured surface into a 3-inch oval. Brush a bit of melted butter on top, then fold the dough in half crosswise.

5. Place one dough portion in the center of a round cake pan and build outward from there, circling the first dough portion and radiating outward until you have 7 rolls. Repeat with a second cake pan and the remaining 7 rolls. Cover with a damp towel and set aside in a warm place to proof for 1½ hours. Meanwhile, preheat the oven to 350°F (175°C) with a rack in the middle position.

6. Mix the egg yolk with the milk and brush on top of the rolls. Bake until golden brown, 30 to 35 minutes.

7. Glaze the rolls with the melted butter while still warm and sprinkle with flaky sea salt. Turn out from the pan and enjoy!

# CANAPÉ CRACKERS

MOST people don't take the time to make crackers—and who can blame them? There are countless excellent cracker brands available at grocery stores in every city. However, this book isn't just about reviving outdated recipes like those dreadful aspics from the 1950s; it aims to provide you with simple, approachable recipes that connect to the past.

I promise that if you try making these crackers just once, you'll quickly see why I included them! They are easy to make and serve as a wonderful template that you can modify to suit your preferences. Plus, you can definitely taste the difference, especially when paired with Pimento Cheese (page 72) or Dr Pepper Bean Dip (page 39).  ✦ *Makes about 8 dozen crackers*

3 cups (360 g) all-purpose flour
2 teaspoons (10 g) sugar
2½ teaspoons (13 g) salt, plus more for
    sprinkling

¼ cup (60 g) olive oil, plus more for
    brushing
1 cup (240 mL) water

1. Preheat the oven to 450°F (230°C) with a rack in the middle position. Line a rimmed baking sheet with parchment paper or a silicone baking mat.

2. In a large bowl, sift together the flour, sugar, and salt. Add the oil and water and knead into a dough that is solid but slightly tacky.

3. Chill the dough for 10 to 15 minutes. This will allow the dough to hydrate and rest before rolling.

4. Lightly flour a work surface. Divide the dough in half and roll one piece out $\frac{1}{8}$ inch thick. Using a sharp knife or pizza cutter, cut the dough into your desired cracker shapes. Repeat with the other piece of dough.

5. Working in batches, transfer the crackers to the prepared baking sheet with $\frac{1}{2}$ inch between. Gently brush the tops of the crackers with some olive oil and sprinkle with salt. Bake for 10 to 15 minutes, or until golden brown.

6. Allow the crackers to cool completely on the baking sheet; they will firm up as they cool. Serve immediately or store in an airtight container at room temperature for up to 7 days.

NOTE: *Feel free to add additional seasonings, like fresh or dried herbs, spices, seeds, or even some grated hard cheese along with the dry ingredients.*

# SCOTCH WOODCOCK

**THIS** open-faced sandwich may sound unusual, but it is packed with flavor and offers a delightful retro recipe that will leave people asking for more! Scotch woodcock originates from the UK and is famously served at the Oxford and Cambridge Club as a snack. The anchovy adds a rich umami flavor that blends beautifully with the spices and eggs, creating a truly unique dish. ✦ *Makes 4 servings*

1½ cups (360 mL) milk
2 cups (100 g) panko breadcrumbs
1 teaspoon (5 g) garlic powder
1 teaspoon (5 g) salt
1 teaspoon (2.5 g) ground black pepper
¼ teaspoon (0.6 g) cayenne pepper
¼ teaspoon (0.6 g) ground mustard
3 tablespoons (42 g) unsalted butter

1 teaspoon (5 g) anchovy paste
4 large eggs
4 slices bread, toasted
8 anchovy fillets
1 tablespoon (9 g) capers, fried
   (see Note)
2 tablespoons finely chopped fresh
   parsley

1. In a small saucepan, heat the milk over medium-high heat until it just begins to boil. Turn the heat down to medium-low and add the breadcrumbs, garlic powder, salt, black pepper, cayenne, and ground mustard. Cook, stirring, until thick and smooth, about 3 minutes. Add 2 tablespoons of the butter and the anchovy paste, stir until incorporated, and remove from heat.

2. In a cold sauté pan, melt the remaining 1 tablespoon butter over medium-low heat. Add the eggs and cook, stirring constantly with a silicone spatula, until the curds begin to gather and scramble. Remove from heat when the eggs are soft, custardy, and just set, about 5 minutes.

3. Sprinkle 2 to 4 tablespoons of the breadcrumb mixture on each slice of toast, then top with the scrambled eggs, a couple of anchovy fillets, and some fried capers. Garnish with chopped parsley and serve right away.

**NOTE:** *To fry the capers, drain them and dry on paper towels. Add to a small saucepan with about 1 cup of olive oil and place over medium high heat. Cook until crispy and slightly darker in color, about 5 minutes. Remove with a slotted spoon and dry on paper towels.*

# PIMENTO CHEESE SANDWICH

THIS sandwich may seem simple, but it's bold and packed with flavor, much like the South, where it's still a popular option for golf fans at the Masters Tournament in Augusta, Georgia.

Who doesn't love pimento cheese? It's creamy and packs a punch thanks to the hot sauce (traditionally Tabasco brand). It was originally created in New York, where farmers experimented with a soft, unripened cheese later known as cream cheese. The pimento cheese sandwich, on the other hand, was first featured in *The Up-to-Date Sandwich Book* from 1909 and gained popularity as pimento cheese became available commercially a few years later. It quickly became a national favorite for packed lunches, tea parties, and gatherings. However, its popularity diminished after World War II, except in the South, where it remains beloved to this day. ✦ *Makes 6 servings*

½ cup (120 g) cream cheese, softened
¼ cup (58 g) mayonnaise
2 teaspoons (10 mL) hot sauce
1 teaspoon (5 g) salt
½ teaspoon (2.5 g) garlic powder
½ teaspoon (2.5 g) ground mustard

¼ teaspoon (1 g) ground black pepper
1 cup (226 g) drained jarred pimentos, chopped
1 cup (113 g) shredded sharp cheddar cheese
12 slices bread

1. In a large bowl, combine the cream cheese, mayonnaise, hot sauce, salt, garlic powder, mustard, and pepper and mix well with a silicone spatula. Fold in the chopped pimentos and shredded cheese.

2. Taste and adjust the seasoning, then cover and refrigerate until chilled, about 5 hours. The pimento cheese will keep for several weeks.

3. For each sandwich, spread a generous amount between two slices of bread and enjoy!

NOTE: *Pimento cheese is also an excellent dip with Canapé Crackers (page 70) or served sandwiched as a layer in the Frosted Sandwich Loaf (page 78).*

# SLOPPY JOES

THE history of the sloppy Joe is vague, often combining tales of a Cuban bar owner named Jose "Sloppy Joe" Abeal y Otero, who created a variation of what might be considered Cuban picadillo in a sandwich for American tourists around the 1930s. Regardless of how the dish originated, it has become one of my favorite nostalgic meals. ✦ *Makes 4 servings*

1 (8-ounce/227 g) can tomato sauce
¼ cup (60 g) ketchup
2 tablespoons (26 g) brown sugar
2 tablespoons (30 mL) Worcestershire sauce
1 teaspoon (5 g) ground mustard
2 tablespoons (30 mL) olive oil

2 onions, finely diced
4 garlic cloves, finely diced
1 pound (450 g) ground beef or turkey
½ teaspoon (1 g) cayenne pepper
2 tablespoons (36 g) salt, or to taste
4 hamburger buns, toasted
Dill pickle slices, for serving (optional)

1. In a large bowl, add the tomato sauce, ketchup, brown sugar, Worcestershire sauce, and mustard and stir to combine thoroughly.

2. In a Dutch oven or large, heavy-bottomed pot, warm the olive oil over medium heat. Add the onions and garlic and sauté until soft and translucent, 8 to 10 minutes. Add the ground meat, stirring to break up the clumps, and cook until browned, 8 to 10 minutes.

3. Add the tomato sauce mixture and season with the cayenne pepper and salt, then turn the heat down to medium-low, and simmer for 30 minutes. You're looking to gently reduce the sauce a bit and give the flavors time to develop, but if you're pressed for time, it's basically ready to serve once it's warmed through.

4. Top the toasted buns with pickles (if using) and sloppy Joe filling and serve.

# S.O.S.

YOU cannot discuss the history of food in America without acknowledging the impact of the American military. Depending on the decade in question, the military played a significant role in rationing food during wartime, while also introducing soldiers to numerous international dishes during their deployments abroad. These interactions with international cuisine became a catalyst for many dishes that appeared in cookbooks for decades to come. Many American soldiers returned home with fond memories of the meals they had experienced, and their wives would often attempt to recreate these dishes based on the descriptions shared by their husbands.

One of the most iconic dishes still enjoyed today is S.O.S., or "shit on a shingle," known for its simplicity, nutritional value, and low cost in feeding American soldiers. Essentially, it consists of chipped beef served on toast with a béchamel sauce. Whether you served in the Army, Navy, or another branch, you likely enjoyed this dish at some point—and you might want to savor it again now. ✦ *Makes 8 servings*

2 tablespoons (28 g) unsalted butter
2 tablespoons (16 g) all-purpose flour
1½ cups (360 mL) milk, cold
1 (2.25-ounce/64 g) jar chipped beef, rinsed and diced
½ teaspoon (3 g) salt

½ teaspoon (3 g) ground white pepper
¼ teaspoon (0.5 g) cayenne pepper
2 tablespoons fresh thyme leaves
8 slices Buttermilk Bread (page 62) or other bread, toasted

1. In a medium saucepan, melt the butter over medium-low heat. Add the flour and cook for 3 to 5 minutes to remove the raw taste of the flour. When the roux takes on a subtle nutty smell and begins to gently tan, add the cold milk.

2. Increase the heat and bring the sauce to a gentle simmer, whisking constantly to avoid scorching the bottom of the sauce. After several minutes, it will begin to tighten up, making a rich, luscious béchamel sauce. Add the chipped beef and season with the salt, white pepper, cayenne, and thyme.

3. Top each slice of bread with a generous portion of the creamed chipped beef and serve open-faced.

# The FROSTED SANDWICH LOAF

IS it cake? The concept of the "party sandwich" originated from the desire to entertain, nourish, and impress guests. Around the world, there are variations of this sandwich, such as the Mexican *sandwichon* and the Swedish *smörgåstårta*, which are still enjoyed for various holidays and special occasions. Feel free to spread, layer, and decorate your sandwich loaf with your favorite fillings.

The sandwich loaf owes thanks to the introduction of the Pullman loaf in the 1930s, which made sliced bread available to the masses. One could argue that the sandwich loaf is one of the greatest inventions since sliced bread! ✦ *Makes 16 servings*

1 loaf Buttermilk Bread (page 62) or other sandwich bread, unsliced

6 tablespoons (84 g) unsalted butter, softened

1 cup (240 g) Pimento Cheese (page 72)

½ cup (120 g) mayonnaise

½ cup (120 g) tuna salad

4 tomatoes, sliced

Salt and ground black pepper to taste

½ cup (120 g) egg salad

10 radishes, halved and thinly sliced into half-moons

3 or 4 romaine lettuce leaves

12 ounces (340 g) cream cheese

½ cup (120 mL) heavy cream

Chopped fresh parsley, for garnish

1. Carefully slice the loaf of bread lengthwise, rather than crosswise, into five long slices. Liberally spread the softened butter across one side of each slice of bread.

2. Place one slice of bread on a serving platter, buttered side up. On top of the butter, spread half of the pimento cheese and half of the mayonnaise. Add the next slice of bread, buttered side up, and spread the tuna salad across it, then top with tomato slices and a sprinkle of salt and pepper. Add a third slice of bread, buttered side up. Top this slice with the egg salad, half of the radish slices, and the lettuce. Top with the fourth slice of bread and spread with the remaining pimento cheese and mayonnaise, then top with the final slice of bread, buttered side down. Use a few large skewers inserted into the top of the sandwich to hold it together.

3. In a stand mixer or with a hand mixer, combine the cream cheese and heavy cream and whip until light and fluffy, seasoning with a bit of salt to taste. Using an offset spatula or silicone spatula, cover the outside of the sandwich loaf with the mixture until it is completely frosted.

4. Adorn the top of the sandwich loaf with the remaining radish slices running from end to end, along with some parsley. Allow the frosted sandwich loaf to chill in the refrigerator for several hours or overnight to let everything set, then slice and serve.

**NOTE:** *You can also make miniature "sandwich cupcakes" by using a round cutter and creating a tower of smaller shapes in the same way.*

# CHEESE DREAMS

COTTAGE cheese is popular for its great taste, nutritional value, and versatility in cooking. However, I've often struggled to get excited about it. That changed when I tried a wonderful sandwich called the Monte Cristo, which left me craving it and dreaming about eating it.

This recipe for the "cheese dream" sandwich, published in 1954, offers an incredible combination of texture and flavor while also being a highly nutritious meal. The flavor of cottage cheese is quite neutral, so if you, like me, have unresolved childhood feelings about it, I'm here to guide you through the uncertainty. This dish is definitely worth reviving from the past! ✦ *Makes 3 servings*

| | |
|---|---|
| 6 slices bread | ¾ cup (180 mL) whole milk |
| 1 cup (220 g) cottage cheese | 1 teaspoon (5 g) salt |
| Cayenne pepper to taste | 3 tablespoons (42 g) unsalted butter |
| 2 large eggs | |

1. Make three sandwiches with the bread and cottage cheese and a pinch of cayenne on each.

2. Beat the eggs, milk, and salt together in a shallow bowl.

3. Carefully dip each sandwich in the egg batter, using a spatula to gently flip them over to coat both sides.

4. Melt 1 tablespoon of the butter in a sauté pan over medium-low heat. When the butter is melted and the bubbling slows down, add one of the sandwiches and cook for 3 to 5 minutes, or until golden brown. Flip and cook the other side for another 3 to 5 minutes. Transfer to a plate and cook the other two sandwiches in the same way, using more butter. Serve right away.

**NOTE:** *This is a relatively blank canvas of opportunity, so feel free to get creative by adding some pineapple slices or other flavors to make your sandwiches more exciting!*

# SOPHISTICATED CLUB SANDWICH

A sandwich, though humble, can become something much more than just a meal when combined with the right ingredients, setting, and occasion. We've seen this transformation with classic dishes like the Reuben sandwich or the BLT, which have become iconic in American cuisine and are timeless meals enjoyed for generations.

For me, the sophisticated club sandwich has been overlooked in the annals of culinary history and deserves recognition as one of the greatest sandwiches ever made. This is my heartfelt plea for you to try this sandwich at least once—it's a culinary experience worth having for the sake of history. I found this recipe in a copy of *Good Housekeeping's Book of Breads and Sandwiches* from 1958, and I ask that you reserve your judgment until you've given it a taste. ✦ *Makes 4 servings*

16 slices Buttermilk Bread (page 62) or
    other bread, lightly toasted
6 tablespoons (85 g) unsalted butter,
    softened
4 to 8 slices cheddar cheese
4 to 8 slices ham
4 fresh or canned pineapple rings

½ cup (120 g) peanut butter
½ cup (35 g) sweetened coconut flakes
4 tomato slices
12 strips thick-cut bacon, cooked
    until crispy
1 avocado, sliced
Salt to taste

1. Spread each slice of bread with butter.

2. Each sandwich will have 4 slices of bread. For each sandwich, place 1 slice of toast, buttered side up, on a work surface. Add 1 or 2 slices of cheddar, 1 or 2 slices of ham, and 1 pineapple ring. Top with a second slice of toast, buttered side up. Spread 2 tablespoons peanut butter on top and add 2 tablespoons coconut flakes. Add the next slice of toast, buttered side up, and on it add 1 tomato slice, 3 strips of bacon, and one-quarter of the avocado slices. Sprinkle with a pinch of salt. Top with the final slice of toast, buttered side down.

3. Secure each sandwich with toothpicks and cut diagonally into halves or quarters. Serve immediately.

# STUFFED FRANKS

**O N E** of my favorite aspects of collecting vintage cookbooks is the endless creativity authors use to reinvent familiar dishes. Over the years, I've made a variety of unusual recipes that, on paper, shouldn't work—like meringue meatloaf—but surprisingly turn out quite delicious. When I flipped through *Betty Crocker's Outdoor Cookbook* from 1961, I came across a recipe I had to try, and I promise you'll love my variation of it—especially the peanut butter option! Feel free to get creative with other fillings and combinations. ✦ *Makes 6 servings*

6 hot dogs
Shredded cheese, chopped dill pickles,
   and/or peanut butter, for filling
6 strips bacon

6 hot dog buns
Ketchup or mustard, for serving
   (optional)

1. Heat a grill to high heat.

2. Slice each hot dog in half lengthwise, butterflying but not fully cutting into two pieces. Fill each butterflied hot dog with cheese, pickles, or peanut butter and close the hot dog. Wrap each hot dog with a strip of uncooked bacon, curling it around and fastening a toothpick at each end to keep the bacon attached.

3. Grill the hot dogs, split side down, rotating occasionally, until the bacon is crispy and fully cooked, 5 to 7 minutes.

4. Remove the toothpicks and serve the hot dogs in buns, with ketchup or mustard, if you like.

   **N O T E :** *These are best prepared on a charcoal grill, but you can also bake or fry them.*

# MEATS

**WRITING** this chapter was more challenging than you might expect. There are countless amazing dishes I would love to include from the twentieth century, many of which are simple yet packed with flavor. However, when reflecting on the decades, it's important to share recipes that are not only tasty but also relevant and significant. We'll explore budget-friendly meals like the Hotdish (page 88) and the Family Skillet Dinner (page 98), while also highlighting elevated classics such as the Carpetbag Steak (page 99) and my favorite, Boeuf Bourguignon (page 102). Though not every dish has a major historical element, each had a shining moment in the spotlight throughout the century and will feel welcome on your dining table.

Throughout the years of preparing retro recipes in my videos, my favorite aspect has been how cognizant the books were to offer recipes that could be made from leftovers or ways to transform leftovers into something better. My hope, from the selections that I've chosen, is that you adopt a similarly creative approach to using proteins, and to think outside the box after you're finished! Turn the Crown o' Gold Meatloaf (page 93) into a sandwich, or use some leftover steak from the Beef Miroton (page 91) in another recipe. Meat recipes were considered special and were meant to last for days, since it wasn't as easy as it is today to have such abundance. There are thousands of recipes I wish I could've included, but I am quite happy with these fun, obscure, and crowd-pleasing dishes.

# HOTDISH

AMERICAN cooking is truly remarkable. As a nation, we are a melting pot of numerous nationalities and cultures that have shaped our identity. Over the decades, we have refined meals introduced to us through immigration, such as Mexican and various European dishes, adapting them to our own tastes. Among these, one of the most quintessentially American meals is the casserole, with Midwest hotdish standing out as a favorite. It was popularized by Midwesterners of Germanic and Eastern European heritage as a type of goulash for potlucks and gatherings.

Hotdish was first featured in a printed church cookbook in 1930, but it eventually became a staple in many homes during the Great Depression. This was due to its convenience, as it could be quickly made with canned vegetables, cream of mushroom soup, and a protein. Over the years, the classic recipe evolved from using pasta to incorporating the now-popular Tater Tot crust, making it one of the most craveable casseroles I've had the pleasure of enjoying. This recipe captures everything that makes a Midwest hotdish special, but with an even better twist. ✦ *Makes 6 servings*

2 tablespoons (30 mL) olive oil
2 pounds (900 g) ground beef
1 white onion, finely diced
2 celery stalks, finely diced
1 carrot, finely diced
2 pounds (900 g) mushrooms, quartered
1 cup (150 g) frozen peas
1 cup (150 g) frozen corn
2 tablespoons (28 g) unsalted butter
2 tablespoons (16 g) all-purpose flour

1 cup (240 mL) whole milk, cold
1 cup (240 mL) Homemade Chicken Stock (page 225)
Salt and ground black pepper to taste
¼ cup (10 g) fresh thyme leaves
1½ cups (175 g) shredded cheddar cheese
1 (2-pound/900 g) bag frozen potato puffs

1. Preheat the oven to 400°F (200°C).

2. In a Dutch oven or large, heavy-bottomed pot, heat the oil over medium heat. Add the ground beef and cook until browned and most of the liquid is absorbed, 10 to 15 minutes. Transfer to a bowl.

3. Add the onion, celery, and carrot to the fat remaining in the pot and sauté until tender and translucent, about 15 minutes. Add the mushrooms and cook with the other vegetables, stirring occasionally, until the liquid has evaporated and they begin to brown slightly, about 10 minutes. Return the beef to the pot, along with the frozen peas and corn, and turn the heat down to medium-low. Continue to cook while you make the sauce suprême.

*Recipe continues* ➤

4. In a small saucepan, melt the butter over medium heat. Add the flour and cook, stirring, to remove the raw taste of the flour, about 5 minutes. The roux should begin to take on a pale tan color. Add the cold milk and chicken stock, increase the heat to medium-high, and cook, whisking constantly, until the sauce begins to thicken and can coat the back of a spoon. Season with salt and pepper and add the thyme.

5. Add the sauce to the browned meat mixture and mix to incorporate. Transfer the mixture to a 9 × 13-inch baking dish. Top with the cheddar cheese and then add a uniform layer of potato puffs to cover the surface.

6. Bake for about 30 minutes, or until the potato puffs are browned and the casserole is bubbling. Serve hot.

# BEEF MIROTON

GROWING up, I worked on overcoming my strange aversion to leftovers—my parents weren't great cooks and would often scoop anything left the next day onto a plate, cover with plastic wrap and then microwave, which still makes me gag today when I think of it. I discovered later that if I created a completely new recipe using elements from previous meals, it felt exciting and fresh. Often, these new dishes turned out to be much better than I expected because leftovers tend to taste even better the next day. When I eventually made beef miroton, I never looked back; it was both simple to prepare and incredibly delicious. I like to serve it with a bright salad.

*Miroton* translates from French as "boiled meat with onions." This dish has been around since the 1700s and was even one of Marie Antoinette's favorite meals! It gained popularity in the mid-twentieth century as a flavorful and uncomplicated way to repurpose leftovers, whether due to abundance or scarcity. ✦ *Makes 4 servings*

2 tablespoons olive oil

4 onions, finely sliced

1 tablespoon (14 g) unsalted butter

1 tablespoon (8 g) all-purpose flour

1 cup (240 mL) Homemade Chicken Stock (page 225)

¼ cup (60 mL) tomato puree

2 tablespoons (30 mL) champagne vinegar or apple cider vinegar

Salt and ground black pepper to taste

1 pound (450 g) cooked beef, cut into chunks

Leftover cooked vegetables, such as roasted potatoes or broccoli (optional)

½ cup (25 g) panko breadcrumbs

Finely chopped fresh parsley, for garnish

1. Preheat the oven to 400°F (200°C).

2. In a large skillet, heat the oil over medium heat. Add the onions and cook, stirring occasionally, until golden and caramelized, about 25 minutes. Transfer to a bowl.

3. Add the butter to the pan. Once it has melted, add the flour and cook, stirring frequently, until the roux begins to take on a tan color, about 5 minutes. Add the stock, tomato puree, and vinegar and continue cooking until the sauce thickens, 5 to 7 minutes. Season to taste with salt and pepper.

4. Add the beef, caramelized onions, and additional vegetables (if using) to the pan and mix well. Transfer to a 9 × 13-inch baking dish and top with the breadcrumbs. Bake for 10 minutes, or until the breadcrumbs are golden and the casserole is warm and steaming.

5. Garnish with parsley and serve hot.

# CROWN O' GOLD MEATLOAF

◇◇◇◇◇◇◇◇◇◇◇◇◇◇◇◇◇◇◇◇◇◇◇◇ **1950s** ◇◇◇◇◇◇◇◇◇◇◇◇◇◇◇◇◇◇◇◇

AMONG all the unusual retro recipes I've tried over the years, this one continues to surprise me! On the surface, it may seem absurd, but it's genuinely a delicious dish that anyone would enjoy.

This recipe, popularized during the 1950s, gets its name from the addition of yellow mustard in the meringue, which adds a unique twist. The mustard doesn't significantly change the dish's taste or texture, but it does introduce a subtle flavor that complements the meatloaf beautifully. Serve this dish with mashed potatoes and roasted broccoli for dinner, and don't forget to make meatloaf sandwiches for lunch the next day! A classic like this never goes out of style. ✦ *Makes 6 servings*

1 pound (450 g) ground beef chuck
8 ounces (225 g) ground pork
1 green bell pepper, seeded and
    finely diced
2 large shallots, finely diced
1 celery stalk, finely diced
1½ cups (75 g) panko breadcrumbs
¼ cup (60 mL) ketchup

2 tablespoons (30 g) prepared
    horseradish
1 tablespoon (15 mL) Worcestershire
    sauce
4 large eggs, separated
1½ tablespoons salt
1 tablespoon ground black pepper
½ teaspoon (3 g) cream of tartar
2 tablespoons (30 mL) yellow mustard

1. Preheat the oven to 350°F (175°C).

2. In a large bowl, combine the ground beef, ground pork, bell pepper, shallots, celery, breadcrumbs, ketchup, horseradish, Worcestershire sauce, egg yolks, and salt and pepper and mix well. Transfer to a loaf pan or round cake pan and bake for 30 minutes.

3. Using an electric mixer, beat the egg whites to soft peaks, about 7 minutes. Add the cream of tartar and whip until very stiff. Fold in the mustard and spread on top of the hot meatloaf. Bake for an additional 25 minutes, or until the internal temperature is at least 160°F (70°C). Serve hot.

*Meats* ✳ 93

# APPLESAUCE MEATBALLS

TRADITIONALLY, when making meatballs, you prepare a panade, consisting of breadcrumbs moistened with milk. This technique helps keep the meat from drying out. Following this logic, mixing applesauce and cornflakes should work as well—and it truly does.

This dish was more common in the late 1950s when the low-calorie meal trend began to take off and families were seeking healthier cooking options. And I love using cornflakes, as they give great texture and a subtle sweetness that plays nicely with this savory treat. ✦ *Makes 4 servings*

### FOR THE MEATBALLS
1 pound (450 g) ground beef chuck
1 large egg, beaten
¼ cup (60 mL) applesauce
½ cup (30 g) crushed cornflakes, plus more if needed
1 onion, finely diced
1 carrot, finely diced
1 celery stalk, finely diced
3 garlic cloves, finely diced
2 tablespoons (14 g) finely chopped fresh sage
1 teaspoon (5 g) Dijon mustard
1 tablespoon (10 g) salt
1 teaspoon (2 g) ground black pepper
½ teaspoon (1 g) cayenne pepper
½ teaspoon (1 g) MSG (optional)
1 tablespoon (15 mL) olive oil

### FOR THE SAUCE
3 garlic cloves, finely diced
1 (8 ounce/225 g) can crushed tomatoes
1 teaspoon (5 g) sugar
Salt and ground black pepper to taste
5 to 10 fresh basil leaves

### FOR SERVING
Grated Parmesan cheese

1. In a large bowl, combine all of the meatball ingredients except the olive oil and mix well, but take care not to let the mixture tighten up too much. If it feels too loose to form meatballs, add more crushed cornflakes. With an ice cream scoop or wet hands, portion the meat mixture into 1-ounce (30 g) balls (about the size of a golf ball) and place on a rimmed baking sheet.

2. Heat the oil in a large skillet or Dutch oven over medium heat. Working in batches, sear the meatballs until they form a nice crust on the exterior, 7 to 10 minutes. Return the cooked meatballs to the baking sheet.

3. To make the sauce, add the garlic to the fat remaining in the pan and cook over medium heat until fragrant and soft, 2 to 3 minutes. Add the crushed tomatoes, sugar, salt and pepper, and basil and simmer for 10 minutes.

4. Return the meatballs to the pan and braise in the sauce for 20 to 30 minutes, until the meatballs are cooked through. Serve hot, with Parmesan cheese on top.

# PIGS in BLANKETS

I believe that many of the dishes we crave and remember fondly are those that were staples during our childhood and are associated with good memories. When I was growing up in the '80s, my mom often made quick meals that were perfect for us kids to grab while playing outside, and one of our favorites was pigs in blankets. What's not to love about puff pastry wrapped around little sausages that you can eat in a single bite?

But wait until you try this recipe for from the 1953 edition of *250 Ways of Serving Potatoes*. This variation transforms the dish into a more substantial meal by using a baking potato with a hollowed center, which is stuffed with a juicy sausage, baked, and topped with bacon. It's truly incredible!

✦ *Makes 4 servings*

| | |
|---|---|
| 4 russet potatoes, well scrubbed | 4 large sausages, fully cooked |
| Olive oil, for coating | 8 strips thick-cut bacon |
| Salt and ground black pepper to taste | |

1. Preheat the oven to 425ºF (220ºC).

2. Using an apple corer or a knife, hollow out the center of each potato. Liberally coat each potato with olive oil, salt, and pepper. Insert a sausage through the cavity of each potato, then wrap two bacon strips around each potato (or drape the bacon strips over the top with wooden skewers inserted to hold them in place).

3. Place the stuffed potatoes on a rimmed baking sheet and bake for about 45 minutes, or until the potatoes are cooked throughout and the bacon is crispy. Serve hot.

# FAMILY SKILLET DINNER

BREAKFAST for dinner was always my favorite growing up. This delightful twist from the 1960s captured my heart, thanks to the nostalgia it brings and the delicious flavors. Plus, this quick and easy family-friendly meal can be prepared in under 30 minutes.

Spam is a key ingredient in this dish. Originally created in the late 1930s to provide families with affordable protein during the Great Depression, it gained international fame when it was shipped to feed soldiers during World War II and the Korean War. In this skillet dish, Spam adds a wonderfully crispy and salty flavor that keeps you coming back for more. ✦ *Makes 4 servings*

3 tablespoons (45 mL) olive oil

1 (12-ounce/340 g) can Spam, cut into finger-sized wedges

1 large onion, finely diced

2 jalapeño peppers, seeded and finely diced

1 celery stalk, finely diced

½ cup water

2 cups (280 g) frozen hash brown potatoes

5 large eggs, beaten

1 cup (113 g) shredded cheddar cheese

Salt and ground black pepper to taste

Chopped scallions, for garnish

1. Preheat the oven to 350°F (175°C).

2. Heat 2 tablespoons olive oil in a large ovenproof skillet over medium-high heat. Sear the Spam to get a good crust on all sides, 5 to 7 minutes. Transfer the Spam to a plate.

3. Add the onion, jalapeños, and celery to the fat remaining in the pan. Add the water to the pan to deglaze and cook, stirring often, until the vegetables are soft and the liquid has evaporated, about 15 minutes.

4. Add the frozen hash brown potatoes and the remaining 1 tablespoon olive oil and sauté the potatoes with the cooked vegetables for 5 to 10 minutes, until they begin to crisp and color.

5. Remove the pan from the heat. Pour the beaten eggs over the sautéed vegetables, then add the Spam batons positioned around the skillet like the hours on a clock face. Top with the cheese, season with salt and pepper, and bake until the eggs are set and the cheese has melted, about 5 minutes.

6. Garnish with scallions and serve immediately.

# CARPETBAG STEAK

WHEN people ask me about my thoughts on mid-century steak dishes, I immediately think of "surf and turf." Popularized in the 1960s, this dish still remains a common restaurant option today, allowing you to pair a filet mignon or T-bone steak with perfectly seared scallops or a decadent lobster tail. However, the carpetbag steak is rarely mentioned—and this is a mistake.

Dating back to the mid-1800s, the combination of steak and oysters was a staple meal in Swansea, Wales, a working-class village known for its oyster harvest. This dish later made its way to the United States during the California Gold Rush, representing opulence and indulgence, which is reflected in the name "carpetbag"—a pejorative term used to describe someone as opportunistic and greedy. It was a popular menu item during the 1960s and again in the 1990s, but it quickly fell out of favor as it came to be seen as outdated.

Carpetbag steak is truly a unique treat worth trying at home, especially since you're unlikely to find it at your local steakhouse anytime soon. ✦ *Makes 2 servings*

### FOR THE STEAK

3 tablespoons (42 g) unsalted butter

4 button mushrooms, finely diced

1 shallot, finely diced

4 garlic cloves, 2 finely chopped and 2 gently crushed

3 thyme sprigs, leaves picked and stems reserved, plus extra for garnish

3 tablespoons (45 mL) brandy or sherry

4 fresh or smoked oysters, finely diced

2 (8-ounce/225 g) filet mignon steaks

Kosher salt and ground black pepper to taste

2 strips thick-cut bacon

2 tablespoons (30 mL) high-heat oil

### FOR THE SAUCE

1 shallot, finely diced

1 tablespoon (6 g) black peppercorns, coarsely cracked

3 tablespoons (42 g) unsalted butter, cold and cubed

¼ cup (60 mL) brandy or sherry

½ cup (120 mL) beef or chicken stock

¼ cup (60 mL) clam juice or oyster liquor

¼ cup (60 mL) heavy cream

1 teaspoon (5 g) Dijon mustard

1. Preheat the oven to 400°F (200°C).

2. Heat 1 tablespoon of the butter in a large skillet over medium-low heat. Add the mushrooms, shallot, chopped garlic, and thyme leaves and sauté until the liquid released from the mushrooms has evaporated, 5 to 7 minutes. Add the brandy and cook until it evaporates, 5 to 7 minutes. Transfer to a bowl and add the oysters.

*Recipe continues* ➤

3. Cut a pocket in the side of each steak with a small, sharp paring knife, being careful not to cut all the way through. With a small spoon, add the mushroom and oyster mixture to the pocket in each steak, packing tightly. Use several skewers to close the openings. Season on all sides with kosher salt and black pepper. Wrap the bacon around each steak and skewer through the center to hold it in place.

4. Heat a small cast-iron or ovenproof stainless-steel pan over medium-high heat for about a minute, or until water flicked on the surface immediately beads and dances around the pan. Add the oil and place the steaks on top of the hot but not smoking oil. Turn the heat down to medium-low and cook the steaks, rolling them slowly to crisp up the bacon. Using tongs, turn the steaks to the end with the skewers on top and cook for 45 to 60 seconds, allowing a good crust to form, then flip and cook on the skewer side. Add the crushed garlic, thyme stems, and remaining 2 tablespoons butter to the pan and baste the steak for several minutes.

5. Transfer the pan to the oven and bake the steak to your desired doneness, 7 to 10 minutes for medium-rare (120°F/49°C). Transfer the steak to a wire rack or cutting board and let rest while you make the sauce. The steak will continue to cook while resting.

6. Discard the crushed garlic and thyme stems from the pan and pour out all but about 1 tablespoon of fat. Add the shallot and cracked peppercorns and sauté over medium heat for 2 to 3 minutes, until softened. Add the cold butter, whisking as it melts.

7. Either off heat or with caution, add the brandy to the pan and cook until the brandy evaporates. Add the beef stock and clam juice and cook, using a wooden spoon to scrape up any fond (caramelized protein stuck to the pan), until the sauce is reduced by half, about 7 minutes. Add the cream and allow the sauce to simmer until it has reduced enough to coat a spoon, 5 to 7 minutes. Remove from the heat and whisk in the mustard.

8. Plate the sauce and the steak, garnishing with extra thyme if using. Serve at once.

**NOTE:** *This is a hearty dish, as it's high in protein and very filling, so I suggest serving this with lighter sides, like a salad or soup and some roasted vegetables.*

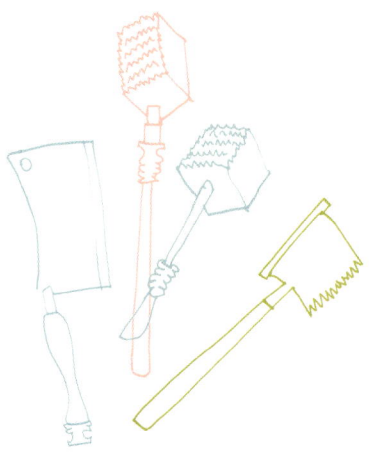

# BOEUF BOURGUIGNON

WITHOUT a second thought, boeuf bourguignon is my favorite dish of all time. It is simply perfect. My first introduction to this dish was through none other than Julia Child's debut cookbook, *Mastering the Art of French Cooking*, published in 1961. While Julia wasn't the first to make this dish or the first to publish a recipe for it, her approach to writing recipes was groundbreaking for that era. She inspired millions of cooks across America to try their hand at French cuisine.

I still salivate at the thought of this dish and vividly remember the first time I made it. After years of preparing this recipe for myself, and for clients as a personal chef, I've realized that I do things a little differently. I usually take extra time to reduce my jus into a rich, rib-sticking concentrate, which makes a significant difference in the end. After making this dish dozens of times, I have perfected my method and find it's muscle memory at this point! Serve with creamy mashed potatoes or polenta to soak up the sauce. ✦ *Makes 6 to 8 servings*

6 ounces (170 g) slab bacon or smoked bacon, cut into ½-inch strips

2 tablespoons (30 mL) olive oil

5 pounds (2.3 kg) boneless beef chuck roast, cut into 2-inch chunks and patted dry

4 tablespoons (32 g) all-purpose flour

2 to 4 carrots, peeled and cut into 1-inch chunks

5 shallots or 2 onions, thinly sliced

2 to 3 tablespoons (30–45 g) tomato paste

1 tablespoon (10 g) salt, plus more to taste

1 tablespoon (6 g) ground black pepper, plus more to taste

1 bottle (750 mL) good red wine, such as pinot noir or cabernet sauvignon

1½ cups (360 mL) Homemade Chicken Stock (page 225)

1 Bouquet Garni (page 229)

2 cups (300 g) pearl onions, root ends trimmed

1 pound (450 g) button mushrooms, stems removed

3 garlic cloves, crushed

6 fresh thyme sprigs

4 tablespoons (56 g) unsalted butter, softened

¼ cup (60 mL) sherry

Chopped fresh parsley and chives, for garnish

1. Preheat the oven to 325°F (160°C).

2. Bring a small pot of water to a boil. Add the bacon and blanch for 3 to 5 minutes. Remove and dry fully with a paper towel, then transfer to a Dutch oven or large, heavy-bottomed pot. Add 1 tablespoon of the olive oil and sauté over medium heat until the bacon is crispy and the fat has rendered. Transfer the bacon to a plate and pour out all but a thin coat of fat from the pot.

*Recipe continues* ➤

3. Dust the beef pieces with 2 tablespoons of the flour. Working in batches, add the beef to the pot and sear over medium-high heat for 5 to 7 minutes, making sure to get a good crust on all sides. Transfer the beef to a rimmed baking sheet.

4. Layer half of the carrots and all of the shallots in the Dutch oven. Put the seared beef on top of the vegetables. Add the tomato paste, salt, pepper, wine, stock, and bouquet garni. Top with a cartouche (see page 226) and bake for 3 to 4 hours, until the beef is tender enough to insert a knife into without effort.

5. While the beef is braising, bring a small pot of water to a boil. Add the pearl onions and simmer them for 4 to 5 minutes. They should still have some crunch, but shouldn't be completely raw. Use a slotted spoon to transfer them to a bowl of cold water. Once they are cool enough to handle, slip off their skins and add the onions to the plate with the bacon. Add the remaining carrots to the boiling water and simmer for 5 to 7 minutes, or until they can be easily pierced with the tip of a knife, then transfer to the plate.

6. Heat the remaining 1 tablespoon olive oil in an ovenproof skillet over medium heat. Add the mushrooms, garlic, and thyme sprigs and season with salt and pepper. Sauté until fragrant, then finish roasting in the oven until fully cooked and the moisture has evaporated, about 10 minutes. Return the pan to medium heat, add 2 tablespoons of the butter and the sherry, and cook until the sherry has fully evaporated, 5 to 7 minutes. Set aside.

7. When the beef is fork-tender, transfer to a heatproof bowl with tongs and add 1 to 2 cups of the hot braising liquid. Strain the remaining liquid in the pot and discard the solids. Wipe out the Dutch oven and return the strained liquid to it. Simmer the liquid over medium-high heat until reduced by half, 10 to 15 minutes.

8. In a small bowl, whisk together the remaining 2 tablespoons flour and 2 tablespoons butter to make a beurre manié. Add half of the beurre manié to the braising liquid and whisk constantly until the sauce begins to thicken, about 5 minutes. Season with salt and pepper. Return the braised beef with the remaining braising liquid to the pot, along with the reserved bacon, carrots, and pearl onions.

9. Garnish with parsley and chives and serve. Bon appétit!

NOTE: *It's important to allow the braised beef to rest in the braising liquid. If you remove the meat and leave it to cool without any of the braising liquid, the meat will be dry and very underwhelming. This recipe is straightforward but requires precision for the best results.*

# POULTRY

**IT'S** almost a universal thing to love poultry, which makes sense, seeing that it's one of the largest industries in the world. As of 2025, there are roughly 26 billion chickens around the globe. A stark contrast to the nearly 8 billion humans that populate Earth!

Poultry is simple to cook and delicious, and takes on flavors so nicely, without having a particularly aggressive flavor, like game or other meats might. Though fowl and wild game have always held a special place at the tables of the wealthiest people in the history books, simple chicken recipes were for the people. It's cheap, healthy, and pretty delicious any way you try to cook it!

Many of the recipes that I included will sound familiar to you, but I made it a point to modify the recipes for our modern palates. Rather than using cream-of-whatever soup as your mom might've done, I'll teach you how to create beautiful French sauces that will offer techniques to unlock hundreds of other dishes. You'll work with fresh herbs instead of seasoning packets or dried flavoring, and you'll be able to tap into the nostalgia of your childhood with ingredients that you can pronounce, without taking the entire day to cook. Many of these dishes were originally made for convenience, but making them better just requires a little more time for a much better product.

I'm very proud of these recipes, and many of them are classics for a reason, but I think you'll find my versions will be just as approachable as they are delicious. Whether you're making the ornate and showy Chicken Buffet in Aspic (page 121) or trying out Country Captain (page 113), America's first curry, you'll find something for everyone and won't regret a thing.

# CHICKEN À LA MARYLAND

MANY of the popular poultry dishes in the United States are as loved today as they were in the past, but one of the lesser-known recipes is the delicious chicken à la Maryland from the turn of the previous century. When people first see this dish, some might give a side-eye to the fried bananas with white sauce and fried chicken, but don't let this unusual combination alarm you. Bananas, you see, were an incredibly popular import through the port of Maryland, and were seen as a luxury item.

Chicken à la Maryland was even served on the first-class menu of the *Titanic* in 1912 and was later adapted by the godfather of French cooking, Auguste Escoffier, who helped create the five mother sauces that we use today! If it's good enough for Escoffier, it's good enough for you and your guests, right? ✦ *Makes 4 servings*

### FOR THE BRINE
¼ cup (72 g) kosher salt
1 quart (1 L) water

### FOR THE CHICKEN
2 large boneless, skinless chicken breasts
1 cup (120 g) all-purpose flour
1 tablespoon (10 g) salt, plus more
　　to taste
½ teaspoon (1 g) cayenne pepper
4 large eggs
1½ cups (75 g) panko breadcrumbs
1 quart (1 L) vegetable oil
4 strips thick-cut bacon, cut into batons

### FOR THE SAUCE
2 tablespoons (28 g) unsalted butter
2 tablespoons (16 g) all-purpose flour
1 cup (240 mL) milk
1 cup (240 mL) Homemade Chicken Stock
　　(page 225)
1 tablespoon (3 g) fresh thyme leaves
Salt to taste
1 pinch freshly grated nutmeg

### FOR THE BANANAS
3 tablespoons (42 g) unsalted butter
2 or 3 firm yellow bananas, sliced ½ inch
　　thick on the bias

### FOR SERVING
Chopped fresh greens

1. To make the brine, combine the kosher salt and water in a container. Add the chicken and brine overnight in the refrigerator. When ready to cook, remove the chicken from the brine and rinse well.

2. Prepare a breading station with three shallow dishes. In the first, whisk together the flour, salt, and cayenne. In the second, whisk the eggs. Put the breadcrumbs in the third.

*Recipe continues* ➤

3. Butterfly each chicken breast and pat dry. Dredge them first in the seasoned flour, then transfer to the egg wash, and then to the breadcrumbs. Make sure that there aren't any dry patches of flour after the egg wash. If you find dry patches, return to the egg wash before coating in breadcrumbs. Transfer to a rimmed baking sheet.

4. In a Dutch oven or large, heavy-bottomed pot, heat the oil to 350°F (175°C). Set a rack in a rimmed baking sheet. Add the bacon to the oil and fry until crispy, 7 to 10 minutes; use a slotted spoon to transfer to a plate lined with paper towels. Working in batches, add the chicken to the oil and fry until the breading is golden brown and the internal temperature reaches 165°F (75°C), 7 to 10 minutes; transfer to the rack and season with salt on both sides while hot.

5. To make the sauce, in a medium saucepan, melt the butter over medium heat. Add the flour and cook, whisking occasionally, for about 4 minutes, until the roux is a light tan color. Add the milk, stock, and thyme, turn the heat up to medium-high, and whisk until the sauce thickens, 5 to 7 minutes. Season with salt and nutmeg.

6. To make the bananas, in a medium sauté pan, melt the butter over medium heat. Add the bananas and cook until golden brown on both sides, 7 to 10 minutes.

7. To serve, slice the fried chicken and plate. Dress the chicken with a generous ladle of the sauce. Top with the fried bananas, crispy bacon, and chopped greens.

# CHICKEN À LA KING

LIKE many of the recipes I researched for this book, the exact origins of this recipe are soft at best, but the name "chicken à la King" is likely familiar to all. The strongest source leads to the story of Bill King, a chef in the 1890s who worked at the Bellevue Hotel in Philadelphia. Upon his death in 1915, his headstone read: *"The name of William King is not listed among the great ones of the earth. No monuments will ever be erected to his memory, for he was only a cook. Yet what a cook! In him blazed the fire of genius which, at the white heat of inspiration, drove him one day, in the old Bellevue, in Philadelphia, to combine bits of chicken, mushrooms, truffles, red and green peppers and cream in that delight-some mixture which ever after has been known as "'Chicken à la King.'"*

In this recipe, I have added a vol-au-vent puff pastry, which allows you to fill each pastry parcel with the delicious, creamy filling, topped with a pastry hat. ✦ *Makes 6 servings*

4 tablespoons (56 g) unsalted butter
1 onion, finely diced
2 celery stalks, finely diced
4 carrots, finely diced
3 garlic cloves, finely diced
1 pound (450 g) mushrooms, quartered
¼ cup (60 mL) sherry
2 tablespoons (16 g) all-purpose flour
2½ cups (600 mL) Homemade Chicken Stock (page 225)

½ cup (120 mL) heavy cream
¼ cup (6 g) chopped fresh thyme
3 cups (420 g) chopped cooked chicken
½ cup (75 g) frozen green peas
3 tablespoons (45 g) diced jarred pimentos
Salt and ground black pepper to taste
12 frozen vol-au-vent puff pastry shells, baked according to package instructions

1. In a Dutch oven or other large, heavy-bottomed pot, heat 2 tablespoons of the butter over medium heat. Add the onion, celery, carrots, and garlic and cook until fragrant, soft, and translucent, 7 to 10 minutes. Add the mushrooms and cook until the moisture is cooked out and they begin to slightly take on some color, 5 to 7 minutes.

2. Add the sherry and scrape the bottom of the pot with a wooden spoon to deglaze. Turn the heat up to medium-high and reduce the mixture until the liquid is mostly evaporated, 5 to 7 minutes.

3. Turn the heat back down to medium and add the remaining 2 tablespoons butter. Once the butter has melted, add the flour and cook, stirring, for 3 minutes. Add the stock, turn the heat up to medium-high, and whisk until the sauce begins to thicken, 5 to 7 minutes.

4. Turn the heat back down to medium and add the cream, thyme, chicken, frozen peas, and pimentos. Simmer for 20 minutes, then taste and adjust the seasoning.

5. Remove the precut pastry center of each vol-au-vent and set aside. Fill each pastry with a generous portion of the chicken mixture and top each with a pastry "hat." Serve right away.

# COUNTRY CAPTAIN

**PERHAPS** one of the most interesting dishes that I'm including in this book, country captain is thought to be one of the first fusion dishes to exist, with lineage directly connecting Indian cooking with British and American ingredients as early as the eighteenth century. It was introduced through the Southern ports of Savannah and Charleston and was even a personal favorite meal for General George Patton, after this dish was served to him and President Franklin Roosevelt in the 1930s. This launched the dish into military popularity among army wives and it was eventually nationally recognized in the 1950s when it was published in *The Joy of Cooking* and notable Southern cookbooks.

The complexity of the aromatics, blended with the sweetness of almonds, raisins, and coconut, make this dish exciting, hearty, and perfect for the cooler months of the year. Despite the lengthy ingredient list, it's simpler to make than you might think. ✦ *Makes 4 servings*

1 tablespoon (7 g) Madras curry powder
1 tablespoon (10 g) kosher salt, plus
    more to taste
¼ teaspoon (0.5 g) cayenne pepper
8 bone-in, skin-on chicken thighs,
    trimmed of excess fat and skin
6 strips thick-cut bacon, cut into batons
¼ cup (60 mL) water
2 onions, finely diced
1 bell pepper, any color, seeded and
    finely diced
1 large jalapeño pepper, seeded and
    finely diced
6 garlic cloves, finely diced

1 (2- to 3-inch) knob ginger, peeled and
    finely diced
1 (28-ounce/794 g) can crushed
    tomatoes
1 tablespoon apple cider vinegar
½ cup (120 mL) Homemade Chicken
    Stock (page 225)
½ cup (75 g) golden raisins
1 tablespoon (13 g) coconut oil
½ cup (70 g) slivered almonds
½ cup (40 g) sweetened coconut flakes
1 tablespoon (8 g) coriander seeds
1 tablespoon (6 g) cumin seeds
¼ cup (6 g) chopped fresh cilantro
¼ cup (6 g) chopped fresh parsley

1. Preheat the oven to 325°F (160°C) with a rack in the middle position.

2. Combine 1½ teaspoons of the curry powder with the salt and cayenne and rub the mixture into the chicken thighs. Set aside.

3. In a Dutch oven or large, heavy-bottomed pot, cook the bacon in the water over medium heat until the bacon is crispy, 7 to 10 minutes. Transfer the bacon to a paper towel–lined plate. Add the chicken to the pot, skin-side down, and cook until the skin is crispy and golden, 7 to 10 minutes. Transfer the chicken to a rimmed baking sheet. Pour out all but about 2 tablespoons fat from the pot.

*Recipe continues* ➤

4. Add the onions, bell pepper, jalapeño, garlic, and ginger to the pot and sauté until fragrant, 7 to 10 minutes. Add the crushed tomatoes, vinegar, and stock and cook for another 10 minutes. Using an immersion blender, briefly pulse the blades in the liquid to break up the vegetables.

5. Add the raisins, reserved bacon, and chicken to the pot, resting the chicken on top and skin-side up, above the sauce. Transfer the pot to the oven and cook for about 45 minutes, or until the chicken is golden and cooked through.

6. In a medium sauté pan, heat the coconut oil over medium heat. Add the almonds and coconut and cook until fragrant and lightly golden in color, 4 to 5 minutes. Remove from the heat and add the coriander and cumin seeds, a pinch of salt, and the remaining curry powder. Toss to thoroughly combine.

7. Transfer the braised chicken to a platter. Add the cilantro and parsley to the sauce, and spoon on top of the chicken. Top each portion of chicken with some coconut-almond crumble and any extra herbs and serve.

# CHICKEN KIEV

WHEN I was growing up in the '80s, my family often cooked frozen meals that were convenient and inexpensive to make. Chicken Kiev (aka chicken Kyiv or côtelette de volaille) was one of my favorites and is still special today for the nostalgia it gives me.

The dish itself is quite old, originating sometime around the eighteenth century in Eastern Europe, but it gained popularity in America around the end of World War II, when restaurants in New York City began to serve "chicken cutlet à la Kiev," with the local press writing warnings about the dangers that this dish presented to the clothing of careless diners. If you know, you know. Shortly after that, commercially available frozen meals began to take the country by storm, and chicken Kiev became a staple in many households for decades to follow. Serve with whipped potatoes or polenta and a side of vegetables. ✦ *Makes 2 servings*

**FOR THE BRINE**
¼ cup (72 g) kosher salt
1 quart (1 L) water

**FOR THE CHICKEN**
2 large boneless, skinless chicken breasts
6 tablespoons (84 g) unsalted butter, softened
4 garlic cloves, finely diced
½ shallot, finely diced

3 tablespoons (12 g) finely chopped fresh parsley
1 cup (120 g) all-purpose flour
1 tablespoon (10 g) salt, plus more to taste
½ teaspoon (1 g) cayenne pepper
4 large eggs
1½ cups (75 g) panko breadcrumbs
4 cups (1 L) vegetable oil
Finely chopped chives, for garnish (optional)

1. To make the brine, combine the kosher salt and water in a container. Add the chicken and brine overnight in the refrigerator.

2. In a food processor, combine the softened butter, garlic, shallot, and parsley and pulse until fully blended. Transfer to a sheet of plastic wrap and roll into a log. Chill in the refrigerator for at least 30 minutes while you prepare the chicken.

3. Remove the chicken from the brine, rinse, and pat dry. Remove the chicken tenderloins, if attached, and flatten each breast between two pieces of plastic wrap or parchment paper using a meat mallet, rolling pin, or small, heavy skillet until about ½ inch thick.

4. Divide the compound butter in half and add half to the center of each flattened chicken breast. Overlap any thin portions of the chicken over the butter and fold the breast over so the butter is completely covered. Wrap each chicken breast in plastic wrap and freeze for about 30 minutes so that they firm up but aren't completely frozen.

*Recipe continues* ➤

5. Prepare a breading station with three shallow dishes. In the first, whisk together the flour, salt, and cayenne. In the second, whisk the eggs. Put the breadcrumbs in the third bowl.

6. Dredge each rolled chicken breast first in the seasoned flour, then transfer to the egg wash, and then to the breadcrumbs. Make sure that there aren't any dry patches of flour after the egg wash. If you find dry patches, return to the egg wash before coating in breadcrumbs.

7. In a Dutch oven or large, heavy-bottomed pot, heat the oil to 350°F (175°C). Add the chicken breasts and fry until the breadcrumbs are golden brown and the internal temperature reaches 165°F (75°C), 5 to 7 minutes. Transfer to a plate and season with salt on both sides while hot. Top with chives, if desired. Serve hot.

**NOTE:** *Be careful when cutting into the hot chicken, as the butter can burst out and burn skin or stain clothing.*

# CHICKEN and BANANA SOUP

1930s

BANANAS are delicious, and in America, we basically view them as an easy snack or something to blend into smoothies, but around the 1930s Big Banana was pushing *hard* to find creative ways to get housewives to purchase more. Cookbooks began to pop up with all sorts of wild recipes educating people on how to prepare banana-based meals, taking inspiration from African and Caribbean influences. But around the early 1950s, a blight swept across North America, wiping out the ever-popular Gros Michel (Fat Mike) banana that was most common.

Have you ever had banana extract and thought "This doesn't quite taste like a banana"? Well, that flavoring is based on the Gros Michel banana! Today we rely on the Cavendish varietal of banana for our daily consumption. It is a wonderfully neutral, less sweet version that lends itself nicely to this recipe.

This simple soup can be made in 30 to 40 minutes and is packed with a sweet and savory quality that is just addictive. ✦ *Makes 4 servings*

2 strips thick-cut bacon, cut into batons
½ cup (65 g) finely diced carrot
½ cup (50 g) finely diced celery
½ cup (60 g) finely diced onion
3 garlic cloves, finely diced
4 to 6 boneless, skinless chicken thighs
4 cups (960 mL) Homemade Chicken Stock (page 225)

1 tablespoon (12 g) brown sugar
½ teaspoon (1 g) cayenne pepper
1 teaspoon (1 g) grated lime zest
1 teaspoon (1 g) chopped fresh thyme
2 ripe bananas
Salt to taste
Finely chopped fresh cilantro, for garnish

1. In a Dutch oven or large, heavy-bottomed pot, cook the bacon over medium heat until the fat has rendered and the bacon is crispy, 7 to 10 minutes. Remove from the pot with a slotted spoon and transfer to a plate. Add the carrot, celery, and onion and cook until the mixture begins to soften and become fragrant, 7 to 10 minutes. Add the garlic and sauté for 5 minutes, stirring occasionally.

2. Add the bacon, chicken thighs, and stock to the pot and turn the heat up to medium-high. Once the liquid comes to a simmer, turn the heat back down to medium. Add the brown sugar, cayenne, lime zest, and thyme and stir to blend.

3. With a ladle, remove about 1 cup of the liquid from the pot and transfer to a blender. Add the bananas and puree. Return the mixture to the pot and simmer for 30 minutes.

4. Remove the chicken from the pot to a bowl. Using two forks, shred the meat. Return to the pot, adjusting the seasoning to taste with more salt or a squeeze of lime for more acidity. Serve, garnished with cilantro.

# TURKEY TETRAZZINI

W H E N I reflect on some of the most popular meals of the mid-century, I find myself once again noticing the power that a casserole had over the nation. We couldn't help but throw everything together and bake it. Named after an Italian opera singer, Luisa Tetrazzini, around 1905, this dish became most popular between the 1950s and 1980s, when many restaurants started adding it to their menus, becoming a common household staple in the 1950s, when frozen dinners became readily available. It's really a fun, tasty, and surprising meal to share with your family, especially using leftover turkey from the holidays. ✦ *Makes 6 servings*

Salt and ground black pepper to taste
1 (12-ounce/340 g) package wide egg
   noodles
3 tablespoons (45 mL) olive oil
1 onion, finely diced
2 celery stalks, finely diced
4 garlic cloves, finely diced
1 pound (450 g) mushrooms, quartered
¼ cup (60 mL) dry sherry
2 tablespoons (28 g) unsalted butter
2 tablespoons (16 g) all-purpose flour
1 cup (240 mL) milk

½ cup (120 mL) Homemade Chicken
   Stock (page 225)
1 large egg yolk
1 tablespoon (6 g) red pepper flakes
2 cups (300 g) chopped cooked turkey
   or chicken
¼ cup (6 g) finely chopped fresh sage
½ cup (25 g) panko breadcrumbs
   (optional)
½ cup (70 g) slivered almonds
¼ cup (12 g) finely chopped fresh parsley

1. Preheat the oven to 375°F (190°C).

2. Bring a large pot of salted water to a boil. Add the egg noodles and cook according to the package instructions until al dente. Drain and toss with 1 tablespoon of the olive oil. Set aside.

3. In a large ovenproof skillet, heat the remaining 2 tablespoons olive oil over medium heat. Add the onion, celery, and garlic and sauté until fragrant and translucent, 7 to 10 minutes. Add the mushrooms and cook until most of the liquid has been cooked out, 5 to 7 minutes. Deglaze the pan with the sherry, turn the heat up to high, and cook, scraping the pan, until the liquid is reduced to about 1 tablespoon.

4. Turn the heat down to medium-low and add the butter. Once the butter has melted, add the flour and cook, stirring, for 3 minutes. Add the milk and stock and whisk until the sauce thickens, 5 to 7 minutes. Remove from the heat and add the egg yolk and red pepper flakes, whisking constantly for about 1 minute to emulsify the sauce.

5. Add the egg noodles, turkey, and sage, stir to combine, and adjust seasoning with salt and black pepper. Top with the breadcrumbs (if using) and almonds.

6. Bake for about 20 minutes, until hot. Allow to cool for 5 minutes, then garnish with parsley and serve.

# CHICKEN BUFFET in ASPIC

RETRO Recipes Kitchen was started in the early months of 2021, after Keiko and I moved from NYC to South Florida, and the second video I ever made was this chicken buffet in aspic recipe. Despite the fact that it was not my favorite thing to eat, it was so fun to make and ultimately was directly responsible for growing my audience with over 6 million views!

Aspics have existed for hundreds of years, and are still commonly enjoyed by millions around the world. Though they never really landed steadily for my palate, I do love to make them. This version incorporates some of the natural gelatin found in Homemade Chicken Stock (page 225) plus some powdered gelatin to really get that wobble we all want.

I mean, it's basically a soup that can stand up, so what's not to love, right? Well, according to my studies, aspics in America were viewed more as ornate tablescapes that were meant to wow your guests, rather than an edible side dish. Whether you eat it or not, I'd be remiss if I didn't include the dish that launched my career as a cookbook author. ✦ *Makes 8 servings*

| | |
|---|---|
| 2 boneless, skinless chicken breasts | ½ cup (120 mL) cold water |
| 1 onion, quartered | 6 (¼-ounce/42 g) packets unflavored |
| 1 bay leaf | gelatin |
| 4 cups (950 mL) Homemade Chicken | 1 cup (150 g) frozen peas, thawed |
| Stock (page 225) | ½ cup (100 g) jarred pimento peppers |
| 2 large egg whites | ½ cup (70 g) pitted black olives |

1. In a large pot, combine the chicken, onion, bay leaf, and stock. Bring to a boil, then turn the heat down to medium-low and poach the chicken until it is fully cooked, 10 to 15 minutes. Remove the chicken and cool. Strain the liquid into a clean bowl, reserving the liquid but discarding the onion and bay leaf. When the chicken is cool enough to handle, cut it into bite-size pieces.

2. Using an electric mixer, beat the egg whites to soft peaks, about 5 minutes. Return the stock to the pot, add the whipped egg whites, and bring to a boil. Boil for 3 minutes, then turn the heat down to medium-low and allow the stock to simmer for 30 to 40 minutes. The egg whites will act as a filter to remove impurities in the stock, making it clearer. With a ladle, break through the egg white "raft" and carefully ladle the clarified stock into a clean bowl. Alternatively, you can pour the contents of the pot through a fine-mesh strainer lined with cheesecloth.

3. Put the cold water in a shallow bowl. Sprinkle the gelatin evenly over the top of the water and allow to bloom for 5 minutes. Add the bloomed gelatin to the warm liquid, whisking to dissolve.

*Recipe continues* ➤

4. Fill a large bowl with crushed ice and place a 6-cup (1.4 L) gelatin mold in it to chill the outside. Spray the mold with a bit of nonstick spray. Add about $\frac{1}{4}$ cup of the gelatin broth to the mold. The aspic will begin to set in the ice water bath, allowing you to layer the ingredients however you like. You are essentially building the aspic upside down. Create layers of chicken, peas, pimentos, and olives, adding more aspic with each addition and allowing it to set in the ice bath. Continue layering until the entire mold has been filled, then refrigerate until fully set, at least 6 hours or overnight.

5. To unmold, gently shake the mold backward and forward until you begin to see the aspic pull away from the edges, rotating and repeating around the entire mold. This will break the vacuum in the mold, letting the aspic release more easily. Then dip the bottom of the mold in warm water for 10 seconds to help loosen. Place a large plate over the open base of the mold and invert. Refrigerate for 1 more hour before serving.

# CHICKEN DIVAN

CHICKEN divan is regularly featured in most of the mid-century cookbooks I've collected. And what's not to love about tender chicken cooked with broccoli and cheese and a topping of crushed Ritz crackers? As it turns out, the recipe was created as a competition entry in the early 1900s by Anthony Lagasi for the Divan Parisien Restaurant, which was located inside the famed Chatham Hotel in New York City.

It's great as is, but we can improve upon this retro favorite by roasting the broccoli to give it more robust flavor and a better texture. ✦ *Makes 6 servings*

4 cups (480 g) frozen broccoli florets
4 tablespoons (30 mL) olive oil
Salt and ground black pepper to taste
2 large boneless, skinless chicken breasts
2 cups (480 mL) water
1 onion, finely diced
1 celery stalk, finely diced
1 carrot, finely diced
4 garlic cloves, finely diced
2 tablespoons (28 g) unsalted butter

2 tablespoons (16 g) all-purpose flour
1½ cups (360 mL) milk
½ cup (120 mL) heavy cream
¼ cup (10 g) chopped fresh thyme
1 large egg yolk
2½ cups (300 g) shredded cheddar cheese
½ cup (60 g) crushed butter crackers or panko breadcrumbs
Finely chopped fresh parsley, for garnish

1. Preheat the oven to 400°F (200°C).

2. Scatter the frozen broccoli florets in a single layer on a rimmed baking sheet. Drizzle with 2 tablespoons of the olive oil and season with salt, then roast for about 20 minutes, or until the florets have a nice bit of caramelization on the edges. Turn the oven temperature down to 350°F (170°C).

3. Combine the chicken and water in a medium saucepan over medium-low heat and poach the chicken for 10 to 15 minutes. Strain, cool, and cut into bite-size pieces, then put in a 2-quart (2 L) casserole dish or Dutch oven. Add the broccoli.

4. In a large skillet, heat the remaining 2 tablespoons olive oil over medium heat. Add the onion, celery, carrot, and garlic and sauté until fragrant and translucent, 7 to 10 minutes. Add the sautéed vegetables to the chicken and broccoli.

5. In a small saucepan, melt the butter over medium heat, add the flour and cook for 3 minutes. Add the milk, cream, and thyme. Turn the heat up to medium-high and cook, whisking, until the sauce thickens, 5 to 7 minutes. Remove from the heat, add the egg yolk, and whisk constantly for about 30 seconds until emulsified and rich. Stir in the shredded cheese and return to medium heat to melt the cheese.

6. Add the sauce, tossing to combine thoroughly. Season to taste with salt and pepper and top with the crackers. Bake for 8 to 10 minutes, until the crackers are golden and the filling is bubbly. Garnish with parsley and serve.

# SEAFOOD

**IN** the past, recipes for seafood often called for canned fish mixed with various other ingredients, resulting in dishes that made you forget you were eating fish altogether. I wanted to create recipes for both fish and shellfish that honored the ingredients and inspired you to cook!

I'd be lying if I said this wasn't the hardest chapter to write in the entire book. Seafood, as it appears in my vast collection of cookbooks, has never seemed particularly appetizing to me. Many of the recipes were either incredibly dull or completely overwhelmed by ingredients like mayonnaise and gelatin that sent me running in the opposite direction. I was determined to right this in *Retro Recipes*, because seafood is a beautiful ingredient that deserves respect, attention, and plenty of seasoning.

In this chapter, we'll tackle some timeless classics like Clams Casino (page 130), explore the wonderful world of casseroles with Tuna Noodle Casserole (page 139), and even introduce some of my personal favorites, such as the Hangtown Fry (page 136)—a dish that is a delightful explosion of texture and flavor that I often dream about making.

We will show our ancestors how close they might've come, when they dropped the ball. We'll think of them while enjoying these delicious dinners, knowing they tried their best—and it wasn't enough. Because seafood is a beautiful thing, a sacred thing, and it's not fair that the coasts of the country got it right and the rest of the country had to mix lemon-lime Jell-O to get through. But I promise that whether you're from the coastal town of Portland, Maine, or landlocked Nashville, Tennessee, you'll cook delicious seafood recipes that would get the thumbs-up from grandmas around the world.

# BONAC CLAM PIE

WHEN I think of clams, my brain instantly fills in "chowder" to follow. Though clams are known for many other wonderful dishes, I was pleased to discover the Bonac clam pie, which is a perfect hybrid of a clam chowder and a fish pie together!

"Bonac" is short for the last name of the original settlers of eastern Long Island, the Bonackers, and this dish was originally created around the mid-1600s. Though clams were common across the Eastern seaboard, this was a dish commonly found around the East End of Long Island, New York. Native Americans taught the settlers how to rake for clams while bartering for goods. This rustic dish was seen as a lowly peasant dish reserved for fishermen and laborers, but the joke is on everyone else because this pie is incredible. ✦ *Makes 8 servings*

### FOR THE PIE CRUST
2½ cups (300 g) all-purpose flour
1 cup (225 g) unsalted butter, frozen
    and grated
1 teaspoon (5 g) salt
1 teaspoon (5 g) sugar
¼ to ½ cup (60–120 mL) ice water

### FOR THE FILLING
2 russet potatoes, scrubbed and
    diced small
2 tablespoons (28 g) unsalted butter
1 onion, finely diced

1 celery stalk, finely diced
4 garlic cloves, finely minced
2 tablespoons (15 g) all-purpose flour
1 cup (240 mL) milk
½ cup (120 mL) clam juice
3 dozen clams, shucked
3 tablespoons (9 g) chopped fresh thyme
¼ teaspoon (0.5 g) cayenne pepper
Salt and ground black pepper to taste

### FOR ASSEMBLY
2 large eggs, beaten

1. Make the pie crust: Combine the flour, frozen butter, salt, and sugar in a food processor and pulse to chop until you have pea-size butter chunks. Slowly add the ice water through the feed tube, pulsing until the dough comes together. Divide the dough in half, wrap each portion in plastic wrap, and refrigerate for 30 minutes to chill the butter.

2. While the dough is chilling, bring a medium pot of water to a boil. Add the potatoes and cook until fork-tender but not falling apart, about 12 minutes. Drain.

3. Meanwhile, in a medium sauté pan, melt the butter over medium heat. Add the onion, celery, and garlic and cook until the onion is translucent, about 8 minutes. Stir in the flour and cook for 5 minutes to remove the raw flour taste, but do not let it darken. Add the milk and clam juice and cook, whisking until thickened slightly, 5 to 7 minutes. Add more liquid if necessary for the right consistency. Add the potatoes, clams, thyme, and cayenne and season with salt and black pepper. Remove from the heat.

4. Preheat the oven to 375°F (190°C).

5. On a lightly floured work surface, roll out one portion of dough to $\frac{1}{8}$-inch thickness. Repeat with the other portion of dough.

6. Place one crust in a 9-inch pie pan, pressing it gently into the corners. Fill with the clam mixture, then top the pie with the second crust. Crimp the edges all around and cut a few vents to allow steam to escape. Brush with the beaten eggs and allow to dry for 5 minutes.

7. Bake for 40 minutes, or until golden brown on top and fully cooked inside. Allow to cool for 10 minutes before serving.

# CLAMS CASINO

AT the turn of the twentieth century, the food trend among the finest hotels, restaurants, and casinos across the United States was to create a baked shellfish dish as a signature menu item. This trend faded fairly rapidly, with the exception of clams casino and Oysters Rockefeller (page 135), which are still enjoyed today, over a hundred years later.

But, like many of the recipes in this book, the true origin of this recipe is difficult to confirm, as much of our culinary history is simply based on lore, rumor, and educated guessing. The prevailing theory is that clams casino was created at the Little Casino in Narragansett, Rhode Island, in 1917, for a client who wanted a special dish to impress her guests. The chef cooked some local clams, topped them with bacon and breadcrumbs, and the rest is history.

My version of this recipe improves upon the common flaws that the dish often suffers from, like sandy breadcrumbs and an overall imbalance of flavors. We'll concentrate them with some culinary technique that not only will make this easy to replicate but can be done ahead of time!

✦ *Makes 8 servings*

4 strips bacon, finely diced
¼ cup (60 mL) water
1 cup (50 g) panko breadcrumbs
3 large shallots, finely diced
3 medium garlic cloves, finely minced
Pinch red pepper flakes
¼ cup (60 mL) dry white wine

Juice of ½ lemon
24 littleneck clams, purged (see Note)
1 cup (225 g) unsalted butter, softened
½ cup (30 g) minced fresh parsley
Grated zest of 1 lemon
Salt and ground black pepper to taste

1. Combine the bacon and water in a medium sauté pan and cook over medium heat until the fat has rendered out and the bacon has become crispy, 10 to 15 minutes. Using a slotted spoon, transfer the bacon to a bowl.

2. Pour half of the fat remaining in the pan into a large sauté pan. Add the breadcrumbs to the smaller pan and gently toast over medium heat until golden, 5 to 7 minutes; remove from the heat. In the large pan, cook the shallots and garlic over medium heat until softened and fragrant but not browned, 7 to 10 minutes. Add the pepper flakes, white wine, lemon juice, and clams. Turn the heat up to medium-high, cover the pan, and cook until the clams begin to open, 5 to 7 minutes. As the clams open, transfer them to a rimmed baking sheet and remove the top shell from each clam. Discard any clams that fail to open. Continue to cook until the clam liquor and wine mixture has entirely reduced, leaving a pulpy shallot mixture, 5 to 7 minutes.

*Recipe continues* ➤

3. In a large bowl, combine half of the reserved bacon, the shallot paste, softened butter, and half of the parsley and mix well. Spread the compound butter generously over each clam. (You will have plenty of compound butter left over, so reserve it for another use.)

4. In another bowl, combine the toasted breadcrumbs, the remaining bacon, and half of the lemon zest and mix well. Top each dressed clam with a sprinkle of the breadcrumb mixture. The clams can be prepared to this point ahead of time, covered, and stored in the refrigerator for up to 2 days.

5. When ready to cook, preheat the oven to 450°F (230°C) with a rack in the middle position.

6. Arrange the clams on a baking sheet, with crumpled aluminum foil to help hold the shells upright. Bake the clams for 3 to 5 minutes, or until the butter is bubbling and the tops begin to gently brown. Remove from the oven, garnish with the remaining parsley and lemon zest, and serve hot.

NOTE: *To purge the clams, in a large pot, dissolve 2 tablespoons (36 g) kosher salt in 1 quart (1 L) water. Scrub the clams, then submerge them in the brine for at least 2 hours at cool room temperature or overnight in the refrigerator. Lift the clams from the pot, leaving the sand and grit behind. Rinse the clams under cold running water before cooking. Discard any open clams that don't close when gently tapped.*

# LOBSTER THERMIDOR

LOBSTER thermidor is one of the most famous dishes, yet its documented history is surprisingly obscure. Some believe it was served to Napoleon Bonaparte during the month of Thermidor (July, according to the French Republican calendar). Others suggest it was created as a tribute to a controversial French play titled *Thermidor*. Regardless of its origins, there's no denying how fantastic this dish is.

Over the last two hundred years, the recipe has evolved, but the classic mid-century version typically included mushrooms, cream, cheese, and brandy. This rendition is presented in split lobster shells, creating a visually stunning display that is sure to make your guests feel like an emperor for a day. ✦ *Makes 4 servings*

### FOR THE COURT BOUILLON

3 cups (720 mL) dry white wine
1 large onion, finely diced
1 large carrot, finely diced
1 celery stalk, finely diced
2 garlic cloves, crushed
6 fresh parsley sprigs
1 tablespoon (3 g) chopped fresh thyme
2 fresh tarragon sprigs, chopped
1 star anise
1 bay leaf
4 (2-pound/900 g) live lobsters

### FOR THE FILLING

10 tablespoons (140 g) unsalted butter
1 pound (450 g) mushrooms, quartered
1 teaspoon (5 mL) lemon juice
1 teaspoon (5 g) salt, plus more to taste
¼ cup (32 g) all-purpose flour
1 teaspoon (5 g) Dijon mustard
3 to 6 tablespoons (45–90 mL) heavy
    cream
¼ cup (60 mL) cognac
½ cup (50 g) grated Parmesan cheese
Chopped fresh parsley, for garnish
Lemon wedges, for serving

1. In a very large pot, combine all of the court bouillon ingredients except the lobsters. Bring to a simmer over medium heat for about 10 minutes. Turn the heat up to medium-high and bring to a boil. Add the lobsters (if your pot is not large enough, do this in batches), cover, and steam for about 15 minutes, or until the shells turn bright red. Remove the lobsters from the pot and set aside. Strain the court bouillon into a medium saucepan.

2. When the lobsters are cool enough to handle, remove the claws and split the lobsters in half from head to tail. Remove all of the meat from the claws, body, and tail and cut into bite-size pieces; set aside in a large bowl. Remove and discard the intestines and the sacs in the heads.

3. Preheat the oven to 425°F (220°C) with racks in the middle and upper positions.

*Recipe continues* ➤

4. To make the filling, in a medium sauté pan, melt 2 tablespoons of the butter in a large skillet over medium heat. Add the mushrooms, lemon juice, and salt and sauté until the mushrooms begin to sweat their juices, 5 to 7 minutes. Pour any juices released from the mushrooms into the court bouillon pan and continue to sauté the mushrooms until tender, 5 minutes. Transfer the mushrooms to the bowl with the lobster meat.

5. Bring the court bouillon to a boil and reduce until about 2 cups of liquid are left, about 10 minutes.

6. Meanwhile, in another medium saucepan, melt 3 tablespoons butter over medium heat. Once the butter has melted, add the flour and cook, stirring, for 3 to 5 minutes, until the roux is fragrant and light tan. Add the reduced court bouillon and continue to cook, whisking, until the sauce begins to thicken, 3 to 5 minutes. Remove from the heat. Whisk in the Dijon mustard and enough of the heavy cream to reach a consistency that is saucy but not too thin. It should coat the back of a spoon easily.

7. In another sauté pan, melt 4 tablespoons butter over medium heat. Once the butter has melted, add the chopped lobster meat and mushrooms and sauté for about 5 minutes. Add the cognac and cook until reduced by half, about 5 minutes. Add about two-thirds of the cream sauce to the sauté pan and toss to coat everything thoroughly.

8. Arrange the split lobster shells on two rimmed baking sheets, hollowed side up, and spoon the lobster thermidor mixture into each. Sprinkle the Parmesan cheese over each lobster and dot the tops with the remaining 1 tablespoon butter, cut into bits.

9. Bake for 10 to 15 minutes, or until bubbly. Serve immediately, garnished with parsley and lemon wedges.

# OYSTERS ROCKEFELLER

IF there is one dish in this book that is sure to impress, it's oysters Rockefeller. Named after John D. Rockefeller, the wealthiest man in the United States, this luxurious dish embodies his opulence through the use of oysters and a vibrant green salsa verde that symbolizes wealth.

The dish was created in 1889 by Jules Alciatore of Antoine's Restaurant in New Orleans, reportedly due to a shortage of escargot (snails), which were very popular at the time. Jules decided to use local oysters from the Gulf of Mexico, and thus an instant classic was born.

Traditionally, this recipe is made with wilted spinach, but many believe that the original salsa verde was more complex and did not include spinach at all. However, I enjoy using wilted spinach and enhancing the dish with a few other green ingredients. ✦ *Makes 5 servings*

### FOR THE SALSA VERDE
- ½ cup (30 g) baby spinach
- ½ cup (30 g) roughly chopped fresh parsley
- 2 shallots, roughly chopped
- 3 scallions, roughly chopped
- 1 celery stalk, finely diced
- 1 tablespoon (2 g) minced fresh tarragon
- ½ cup (113 g) unsalted butter, softened
- Dash Worcestershire sauce
- Dash hot sauce
- Salt and ground black pepper to taste

### FOR THE OYSTERS
- 2 strips thick-cut bacon, finely diced
- 3 tablespoons (44 mL) water
- ¼ cup (15 g) panko breadcrumbs
- Kosher salt, as needed
- 20 fresh medium oysters, shucked
- ¼ cup (60 mL) heavy cream
- 3 tablespoons (15 g) grated Parmesan cheese
- 1 tablespoon (4 g) finely chopped fresh parsley
- Lemon wedges, for serving

1. Preheat the oven to 400°F (200°C).

2. Combine all the salsa verde ingredients in a food processor and pulse about ten times, or until the greens are chopped and blended with the butter. It should be blended well but not pureed.

3. In a small sauté pan, cook the bacon and water over medium heat until the fat has rendered and bacon is crispy, 10 to 15 minutes. Transfer to a paper towel–lined bowl. Toast the breadcrumbs in the residual fat in the pan until golden brown, 3 to 5 minutes.

4. Spread a generous amount of kosher salt on a large baking sheet. The salt will absorb the heat and hold the oysters upright while cooking. Spoon a generous dollop of the salsa verde on top of each shucked oyster. Pour a small amount of cream into each oyster. Top with the breadcrumbs, bacon, and Parmesan cheese. Nestle the oysters in the layer of salt and bake for 10 minutes, until they're bubbling and the cheese has browned a bit. Garnish with the parsley and serve with lemon wedges.

# HANGTOWN FRY

THE Hangtown fry is one of the most iconic dishes that represent the California Gold Rush, and for good reason. In the 1850s, as settlers journeyed across the United States in search of fortune, a prospector struck it rich in Placerville, California, which was then known as Hangtown. Upon returning to town, he visited the Cary House Hotel and requested the most extravagant meal they could prepare for a hungry man at breakfast.

At that time, eggs were quite expensive due to the challenges of transporting them to the small mining town. The next key ingredient was bacon, which had to be imported from the East Coast to California. Additionally, the kitchen had ice-cold oysters that had been transported over 100 miles from San Francisco. The chef crafted an omelet filled with oysters and topped it with crispy bacon, and that marked the beginning of the Hangtown fry's legacy. ✦ *Makes 1 serving*

| | |
|---|---|
| 1 cup (120 g) all-purpose flour | 4 large eggs |
| 1 tablespoon (18 g) kosher salt, plus more to taste | 1 cup (50 g) panko breadcrumbs |
| 1 teaspoon (3 g) paprika | 1 (3-ounce/85 g) can smoked oysters or 4 fresh oysters, shucked |
| 1 teaspoon (3 g) garlic powder | 2 cups (480 mL) vegetable oil |
| 1 teaspoon (3 g) onion powder | 2 strips thick-cut bacon, cut into batons |
| ½ teaspoon (2 g) ground mustard | 1 tablespoon (4 g) finely chopped fresh parsley |
| ¼ teaspoon (0.5 g) cayenne pepper | |

1. Prepare a breading station with three shallow dishes. In the first, whisk together the flour, salt, paprika, garlic powder, onion powder, mustard, and cayenne. In the second, whisk 2 of the eggs. Put the breadcrumbs in the third.

2. Pat the oysters dry with paper towels. Dredge them first in the seasoned flour, then transfer to the eggs and then to the breadcrumbs. Dredge again if there are any gaps that didn't bind. Set aside.

3. Pour the oil into a medium pot and heat to 350°F (175°C). Using a slotted spoon, carefully lower the breaded oysters into the oil and cook for 3 to 5 minutes, until golden brown. Transfer to a paper towel–lined bowl and season with a pinch of salt.

4. In a medium sauté pan, cook the bacon over medium heat until the fat has rendered and the bacon is crispy, 5 to 7 minutes. Transfer to a plate. Drain off all but 2 tablespoons fat from the pan.

5. Whisk the remaining 2 eggs. Turn the heat down to medium-low and add the eggs to the sauté pan. Season with salt and begin to agitate the eggs with a silicone spatula, moving constantly to avoid overcooking. When the eggs have just barely set, after about 5 minutes, remove the pan from the heat. Insert the spatula under the far side of the omelet and gently fold it over.

6. Transfer the omelet to a plate, garnish with the deep-fried oysters, top with the crispy bacon and parsley, and serve right away.

# TUNA NOODLE CASSEROLE

◇◇◇◇◇◇◇◇◇◇◇◇◇◇◇◇◇◇◇◇◇◇◇◇◇◇ **1950s** ◇◇◇◇◇◇◇◇◇◇◇◇◇◇◇◇◇◇◇◇◇◇◇◇◇◇

ONE of the most iconic casseroles from the 1950s is undoubtedly tuna noodle casserole. It was a staple at every potluck, church garage sale, or funeral, making an appearance almost everywhere. What's not to love? This dish is hot, creamy, and flavorful, made from inexpensive ingredients, and can be frozen and reheated at any time!

There are countless variations of this recipe, reflecting the preferences of those who made it. My version, which uses sauce normande instead of canned cream of mushroom soup, elevates the dish. ✦ *Makes 6 servings*

**FOR THE CASSEROLE**
2 (5-ounce/142 g) cans white albacore
   tuna packed in water
½ (12-ounce/340 g) package egg
   noodles
1 strip thick-cut bacon, finely diced
2 shallots, finely diced
1 celery stalk, finely diced
2 tablespoons (28 g) unsalted butter
1 cup (50 g) panko breadcrumbs
1 cup (150 g) frozen peas
½ cup (50 g) shredded white
   cheddar cheese

**FOR THE SAUCE NORMANDE**
3 tablespoons (42 g) unsalted butter
3 tablespoons (24 g) all-purpose flour
1½ cups (360 mL) Homemade Chicken
   Stock (page 225)
1 pound (450 g) mushrooms, quartered
2 tablespoons (30 mL) lemon juice
1 tablespoon (3 g) finely chopped
   fresh thyme
¼ cup (60 mL) heavy cream
Pinch cayenne pepper
Salt and ground black pepper to taste

**FOR SERVING**
Grated Parmesan cheese
Finely chopped fresh parsley

1. Preheat the oven to 350°F (175°C).

2. Drain the water from the cans of tuna, reserving the water for the sauce. Empty the tuna into a large bowl and break it apart with forks; set aside.

3. Bring a large pot of salted water to a boil and cook the noodles according to the package instructions until al dente. Drain.

4. Meanwhile, in a sauté pan, cook the bacon over medium heat until the fat has rendered and the bacon is crispy and browned, 7 to 10 minutes. Using a slotted spoon, transfer the bacon to a small bowl. Add the shallots and celery to the fat left in the pan and sauté until tender and soft, about 7 minutes. Transfer to the bowl with the bacon.

*Recipe continues* ➤

5. Add the butter to the pan and melt over medium heat. Add the breadcrumbs and gently toast until golden brown, 3 to 5 minutes. Transfer to a separate bowl.

6. To make the sauce, in a medium saucepan, melt the butter over medium heat. Add the flour and cook for 3 to 5 minutes, whisking until the roux turns a pale tan color and bubbles. Add the stock and the reserved liquid from the canned tuna. Turn the heat up to medium-high, whisking until the sauce begins to thicken. Add the mushrooms, lemon juice, thyme, heavy cream, and cayenne and season to taste with salt and black pepper. Reduce until the sauce can coat the back of a spoon, 3 to 5 minutes, then remove from heat.

7. To the bowl with the tuna, add the noodles, frozen peas, cheddar, sautéed vegetables, and bacon, along with enough of the sauce to coat everything. Transfer to a large casserole dish. Top the casserole with the toasted breadcrumbs and bake for 30 minutes, or until bubbling and hot. Top with Parmesan cheese and parsley and serve hot, family-style.

# CABBAGE and COD TIMBALES

MANY people today have likely never heard of a timbale. Essentially, it's a type of vessel used for serving food, with its name derived from the Arabic word *thabal*, meaning "drum" or "drinking cup."

For centuries, these metallic or ceramic molds have been filled with vegetables, forcemeats, and various other ingredients, creating a unique and visually appealing presentation. While they are typically smaller in size, they can also be made in larger forms, such as a Bundt pan or spring-form cake pan.

Timbales gained popularity in the early 1900s but fell out of favor and common use during the Great Depression and World War II. They made a strong comeback on menus and in cookbooks from the 1950s until about the 1970s. These dishes are a delight to see and a real treat to prepare for guests, and not nearly as difficult to make as one might think. ✦ *Makes 4 servings*

### FOR THE CABBAGE
Salt to taste
4 large outer leaves Savoy cabbage

### FOR THE FISH MIXTURE
1 pound (450 g) fresh cod fillets
1 large egg, beaten
1 shallot, finely diced
2 garlic cloves, finely diced
Grated zest of 1 lemon
2 tablespoons (8 g) chopped fresh parsley
2 tablespoons (6 g) chopped fresh chives, plus more for garnish

½ cup (25 g) panko breadcrumbs
Pinch cayenne pepper
1 teaspoon (3 g) cornstarch
½ cup (120 mL) milk
¼ cup (60 mL) heavy cream

### FOR THE SAUCE BÉCHAMEL
2 tablespoons (28 g) unsalted butter
2 tablespoons (16 g) all-purpose flour
1½ cups (360 mL) milk, cold
Pinch freshly grated nutmeg
Salt and ground black pepper to taste
1 large egg yolk

1. Preheat the oven to 375°F (190°C).

2. Bring a large pot of salted water to a boil. Blanch the cabbage leaves for about 30 seconds, or until the leaves are bright green and malleable but not wilted. Immediately submerge the leaves in a bowl of ice water. Squeeze out any excess water and allow the leaves to dry on a rimmed baking sheet lined with paper towels.

3. In a food processor, combine all of the fish mixture ingredients and pulse about 10 times, until you have a thick paste. If too thick, add a touch more milk; if too thin, add additional breadcrumbs, 1 tablespoon at a time, until you've found your desired consistency. There should be some texture and not a completely smooth puree.

4. Lightly grease a 5-ounce (150 mL) timbale mold, deep ramekin, or deep ring mold. Layer the cabbage leaves inside the mold and allow the excess to drape over the sides, so that the inside is completely covered with cabbage leaves. Fill the timbale to the top with the cod mixture and pack it in tightly with an offset spatula or butter knife. Fold the excess cabbage over the top so the cabbage leaves completely surround the filling.

5. Place the mold in a large roasting pan. Pour enough water into the roasting pan to reach halfway up the side of the mold. Bake for 25 to 30 minutes, or until set.

6. While the timbale is baking, make the sauce. Melt the butter in a small saucepan over medium heat. Add the flour and cook, whisking, for 3 to 5 minutes, until the roux is a pale golden tan. Add the cold milk and nutmeg, season with salt and pepper, and cook, whisking, until the sauce is thick enough to coat a spoon, 5 to 7 minutes. Remove from the heat and whisk in the egg yolk for about 30 seconds, until combined.

7. Allow the timbale to cool for 5 minutes and then quickly invert the mold, gently tapping the top. The inside should release easily, as the cabbage-wrapped filling won't stick. Top the timbale with a spoonful of the sauce, garnish with chives, and serve, with the remaining sauce on the side.

# TILAPIA EN PAPILLOTE

THIS recipe is special to me because it comes from Keiko's late grandfather, Ron. He was not only the sweetest man alive but also an exceptional cook who always made sure his guests were well fed and comfortable. His hospitality flowed from him like a summer fire hydrant in New York, and anyone who had the pleasure of knowing him would request this meal for dinner.

The dish is simple, yet it embodies the essence of good cooking by showcasing a few ingredients that complement each other well through excellent technique. Though this dish is personal, it does hold quite a bit of historical relevance. Cooking *en papillote* became popular in the 1960s and '70s, with cooking shows and cookbooks sharing tips and tricks. I would consider this to be one of the earlier "hacks" for home cooks! The method creates steam inside a parchment parcel, which keeps the fish tender and moist. Sometimes, the best food is made with love and cherished memories, and I will always carry Ron's memory with me. ✦ *Makes 2 servings*

1 large onion, julienned
1 red bell pepper, seeded and julienned
1 yellow bell pepper, seeded and julienned
2 tablespoons (30 mL) olive oil
¼ cup (60 mL) water
Salt and ground black pepper to taste

2 large tilapia fillets, patted dry
2 to 4 tablespoons (24–48 g) Old Bay seasoning
2 ripe tomatoes, sliced ¼ inch thick
Leaves from 5 fresh thyme sprigs
1 lemon, zested and quartered
Roughly chopped fresh parsley, for garnish

1. Preheat the oven to 400°F (200°C).

2. In a sauté pan, combine the onion, bell peppers, olive oil, water, and a pinch of salt and bring to a boil over medium heat. Cook until the onion and peppers are tender but not brown, about 10 minutes.

3. Season the tilapia fillets with the Old Bay seasoning.

4. Fold a large piece of parchment paper in half. With a pair of scissors, cut a half heart shape from the bottom of the fold to the top, making it large enough to easily fit the ingredients inside (about 10 inches across). Open the folded paper to reveal a heart shape. Repeat to make a second parchment heart.

5. Divide the sautéed onion and peppers between the two parchment hearts, placing the mixture on one side of the fold and closer to the top third of the heart. Lay the tomato slices on top of the onion and peppers and season with a pinch of salt and pepper. Place the tilapia on top of the tomatoes. Top each with the thyme, lemon zest, and a squeeze of lemon juice.

6. Fold the empty half of the parchment half over. Beginning at the top of the heart, crimp the edges of the two parchment halves together to seal, working your way down the heart. When you reach the bottom, fold the "tail" underneath the parcel so that the weight of the ingredients will hold the parcel together.

7. Place the parcels on a rimmed baking sheet and bake for 12 to 15 minutes. The paper vessel will have some discoloration and toasting and will be quite puffy. The fish will be perfectly steamed inside the parcel.

8. Remove from the oven and either place the parcels on serving plates or open the parcels and transfer the fish and vegetables to plates. Garnish with parsley and an extra wedge of lemon.

# BEVERAGES

FOR nearly fifteen years, I lived in Brooklyn, New York, where I was surrounded by a myriad of cultures and some of the most incredible restaurants in the country, many of which have been around for decades. Some of my favorite memories come from visiting a soda shop called Brooklyn Farmacy, a small restored apothecary shop from the 1920s located in Carroll Gardens. There, I was introduced to the fascinating culture of vintage beverages.

When we talk about old-fashioned drinks, we often default to milkshakes and floats. However, if you dig a bit deeper, you'll discover that the early soda shops created unique beverages, much as bartenders craft cocktails for their patrons! Unique flavors were combined with creamy, refreshing, or effervescent bases, and many shops made their own syrups in-house to attract customers seeking nonalcoholic treats. This is where we begin to see the rise of floats, rickeys, flips, shakes, and even the famous egg cream.

Here are some of my favorite beverage recipes that I've made over the years. I truly hope you enjoy them as much as I do. Many of these recipes include a raw egg, which may seem daunting, but rest assured that our eggs are commonly sanitized. They add a richness to the drink that is simply irresistible. So, prepare yourself for some creamy, fun, cozy, and extraordinary beverages to brighten your day or cap off your evening.

# The CLASSIC NEW YORK EGG CREAM

T O me, there is no better beverage than the classic New York egg cream. That might sound like a bold statement, but when I moved to Brooklyn, I was completely new to the scene. I hadn't even heard of an egg cream before. One summer afternoon, my partner, Keiko, took me to Brooklyn Farmacy, a charming soda shop located in the Carroll Gardens neighborhood of Brooklyn. Their goal was to revive the lost culture of the soda shop, and inside, you'd find dapper "jerks," as they are called, serving milkshakes and malts from open to close. Keiko ordered an egg cream and slid it my way, and the rest is history.

Now, I understand that the name "egg cream" isn't exactly appetizing for a fizzy milk drink, but to say it was "pretty good" would be an understatement—it was an experience. Refreshing, sweet, creamy, and with an exciting tingle from the freshly carbonated water, this is the recipe that popularized the drink in the early 1900s.

The origins of the egg cream are somewhat unclear, but it was popularized by a man named Louis Auster, who moved to New York City around 1890. At that time, soda shops were as common as coffee shops today, with reports of more than seventy soda shops within just a quarter-mile radius in the Lower East Side of Manhattan. Everyone was trying to create unique beverages to attract customers, but it wasn't until Auster experimented with a combination of cocoa, milk, and carbonated water that the landscape changed forever. He named it the "egg cream" to make the drink sound more luxurious, even though it contained neither eggs nor cream, as both ingredients were expensive at the time.

Auster was particularly known for making his own chocolate syrup for the drink and, during the summer months, he would go through 50 quarts of his chocolate syrup every day, producing upwards of three thousand egg creams daily. Around 1903, Fox's U-Bet chocolate syrup was invented in Brooklyn and became the standard for soda shops across the city because it had the perfect taste and dissolved properly in the drink.

The egg cream is an example of restraint in creation. Embrace its simplicity and enjoy every sip. ✦ *Makes 1 serving*

¼ cup (60 mL) milk

¾ cup (180 mL) seltzer water

2 tablespoons (30 g) chocolate syrup

1. In an ice-cold glass, combine the milk and seltzer water, without ice.

2. Pour the chocolate syrup into the center of the glass and gently swirl with the back of a spoon to mix. This will help keep the soda from deflating and will also help mix the syrup.

3. Drink immediately and often.

# HOBOKEN SPECIAL

T H E most challenging part of writing this book has been researching the deep histories behind the recipes. I've often spent hours scouring the internet, reading various books, and comparing notes to ensure I provide the most accurate historical contexts. However, that wasn't the case with the Hoboken special.

I found very little information about it aside from a delightful recipe. This drink is clearly inspired by the New York Egg Cream (page 148), made with syrup, seltzer water, and milk. It seems logical to me that our neighbors in Hoboken wanted to create their own version, and I believe they succeeded brilliantly.

The Hoboken special is bright and acidic, striking a balance between sweetness and the refreshing quality of seltzer water, which keeps it from being overly sweet. I've added a pinch of salt and pineapple syrup to enhance the classic recipe I discovered, adding a depth of flavor that it was previously lacking. ✦ *Makes 1 serving, enough syrup for 4 servings*

FOR THE PINEAPPLE SYRUP
½ cup (120 mL) pineapple juice
½ cup (100 g) brown sugar
Peel from 1 lemon
Pinch salt

FOR EACH DRINK
¼ cup (60 mL) milk
1 scoop (650 g) chocolate ice cream
Seltzer water, to taste
Pineapple wedge, for garnish

1. To make the syrup, combine the pineapple juice, brown sugar, lemon peel, and salt in a small saucepan and simmer over medium-low heat until the sugar has melted and the mixture begins to thicken slightly. Strain the syrup into a clean container and let cool. (The syrup can be stored in the refrigerator for up to 2 weeks.)

2. To make the drink, transfer ½ cup (120 mL) of the pineapple syrup to a blender. Add the milk and chocolate ice cream and blend until smooth.

3. Pour the drink into a tall, cold highball glass or several smaller glasses and top with the desired amount of seltzer water. Garnish with a wedge of pineapple on a skewer and serve.

# CHERRY-LIME RICKEY

DURING the 1920s, when Prohibition banned alcoholic beverages in the US, soda shops gained popularity as an alternative for satisfying the desire for refreshing drinks. One of the most popular cocktails just before Prohibition was the gin rickey, named after Joe Rickey, a lobbyist instrumental in the importation of limes to the country. The gin rickey was modeled after the classic Tom Collins, featuring gin, lime instead of lemon, sugar, and soda water.

After the ban on spirits like gin and whiskey, soda shops began to serve lime rickeys throughout the day. They eventually discovered a delightful combination by adding maraschino cherries and some syrup from the cherry jars, topping it all off with lemon-lime soda. ✦ *Makes 1 serving*

3 maraschino cherries

¼ cup (60 mL) maraschino cherry syrup

3 lime wedges

12 ounces (355 mL) seltzer water or club soda

1. In an ice-cold glass, combine 2 cherries, the cherry syrup, and 1 lime wedge.

2. Completely fill the glass with crushed ice (a food processor makes quick work of this).

3. Top with the seltzer water and squeeze another lime wedge into the glass. Gently tumble with a long spoon or straw to mix.

4. Garnish with the remaining lime wedge and cherry on a skewer.

# BANANA-DATE SHAKE

THE date shake was invented in the 1930s by Russell Nicoll, a date farmer in California's Coachella Valley. He blended his dates into a vanilla milkshake, which became the most popular beverage at soda jerk shops across the country. Before the Cyclone Drink Mixer, an electric blender created by Hamilton Beach in 1910, shakes were often made by hand. The introduction of this tool streamlined the process.

Around the same time, bananas were heavily marketed as an exotic and trendy import to the United States. The Gros Michel banana, known colloquially as "Fat Mike," was the preferred variety back then due to its smaller size and sweeter taste compared to what we consume today. However, in the early 1950s, a blight called Panama disease decimated this variety, leading to a worldwide shift toward the Cavendish banana, also known as the Chiquita banana, which is what we eat today. ✦ *Makes 3 servings*

**FOR THE SHAKE**

**6 pitted dates**

**1 ripe banana**

**Pinch salt**

**4 scoops (260 g) vanilla ice cream**

**1½ cups (360 mL) milk**

**FOR THE GARNISH**

**1 ripe banana**

**Pinch salt**

**⅛ teaspoon vanilla bean paste (see Note)**

**3 pitted dates**

1. To make the shake, combine the dates and banana in a blender and blitz to a thick paste. Add the salt, ice cream, and milk and blend until thick and smooth. Pour the shake into three cold glasses.

2. To make the garnish, mash the banana with the salt and vanilla. Transfer the banana puree to a piping bag and cut off the tip of the piping bag. (Alternatively, you can use a zip-top bag with one corner snipped off.) Fill the dates with the banana puree and add a skewer through each date. Rest on top of each shake and enjoy.

**NOTE:** *I prefer vanilla bean paste to extract because you actually have real vanilla bean seeds and rounder flavors, but in a pinch you can use the same amount of vanilla extract.*

# COWBOY COFFEE

COWBOY coffee is known by many names, including breakfast coffee, Swedish coffee, and church coffee. While it may sound unusual to add an egg and salt to your morning brew, I can confidently say it makes for the best cup of coffee I've ever had.

The process is quite simple. You break an egg into the ground coffee, add water and boil it, and then strain it. This method is similar to making a good consommé or clarified stock, where chefs remove impurities and discoloration from beef stock to achieve a clear liquid. The egg creates a "raft" that captures the coffee grounds while also extracting the bitter tannins from the beans that are released when brewed with heat. The pinch of salt works similarly by softening the acids on our palate, resulting in an exceptionally smooth cup of coffee.

I've prepared this many times, often while camping in remote areas, and I love serving it to my friends. They may put on a brave face at first, but their smiles say it all when they take their first sip, relax their shoulders, and ask for seconds.

The history of cowboy coffee dates back to the cowboys who traversed the United States during the westward expansion. It became popular during the California Gold Rush but saw a decline with the introduction of instant coffee around the 1890s.

If you ever find yourself in need of a hot cup of coffee, keep this method handy. You'll thank me later! ✦ *Makes 4 servings*

¼ cup (60 g) finely ground coffee
1 large egg white
4 cups (1 L) cold water

Pinch salt
Milk and sugar, for serving (optional)

1. In a small saucepan, mix together the ground coffee and egg white into a paste. Add the cold water and bring to a boil. Boil for 3 to 5 minutes.

2. Remove from the heat, cover, and allow to steep for 5 minutes.

3. Strain the coffee from the grounds and add a small pinch of salt, along with any milk and sugar, if desired.

**NOTE:** *It is best practice to ensure that the pot you're using is clean, as coffee has a tendency to absorb flavors and odors very easily. In my experience, using a ceramic or a glass pot is better than a metal pot.*

*If you are using a camping kettle, you should opt for a coarse-ground coffee. Follow the instructions as above, but just before serving, add a splash of cold water to the kettle to force the grounds to sink to the bottom of the pot. This was the more common way of preparing for cowboys in the field who didn't want to worry about straining their coffee grounds, as the egg will bind to the coffee and weigh it down as cold water is introduced to the pot.*

# TOAST TEA

MY favorite chapters in many vintage cookbooks from the 1930s and earlier often include sections titled "Invalid Cookery," which contain recipes designed to care for ill children and adults. Most of these dishes are liquid-based, typically consisting of boiled meats or pureed organs combined with broth, aiming to provide nourishment rather than flavor.

Curious, I decided to try one of these recipes one day, mainly to see how unappetizing it might be. To my surprise, it reminded me of a delicious chicken soup, minus the chicken! It was warm and comforting, evoking nostalgic memories of when I was a sick child and my mom would fix me a can of Campbell's.

While this dish may not transport you back to your childhood memories like Anton Ego in Pixar's *Ratatouille*, it is certainly a fantastic vintage recipe. It can come in handy, especially when you're feeling under the weather. ✦ *Makes 3 to 4 servings*

1 cup (50 g) fresh breadcrumbs
4 cups (960 mL) boiling water
½ cup (120 mL) hot milk

Pinch salt
Crackers, for serving

1. Preheat the oven to 400°F (200°C).

2. Spread out the breadcrumbs on a rimmed baking sheet and bake until toasted and golden but not burnt. This should take only a few minutes, so keep an eye on them.

3. Transfer the toasted breadcrumbs to a small saucepan and add the boiling water. Simmer over medium heat for 10 minutes. Strain and discard the breadcrumbs, retaining the broth.

4. Add the hot milk to the broth and season with the salt. Serve in a warm mug or small bowl with crackers at the ready.

# CATAWBA FLIP

THROUGHOUT my years of creating Retro Recipes, I've developed a deep appreciation for the classic flip, and this particular concoction is definitely worth trying. A flip is essentially a beverage or cocktail that is shaken or blended with an egg or egg yolk. The addition of the yolk provides a creaminess that I haven't found a suitable substitute for.

The Catawba flip dates back to the 1860s, around the time the Welch's company was founded. Traditionally, it is made with grape syrup, but it works wonderfully with a couple ounces of Concord grape juice. The drink is named after the Catawba grape, which was once the most popular grape varietal in the United States. However, by the late 1850s, it was largely replaced by the comparable Concord grape from Massachusetts. In the 1950s, this drink made a comeback as a popular beverage for the warmer months, and for good reason. Enjoy! ✦ *Makes 4 servings*

| | |
|---|---|
| 1 scoop (65 g) vanilla ice cream | ½ cup (about 70 g) ice |
| 1 large egg | Pinch salt |
| ¼ cup (60 mL) grape juice | Seltzer water, to taste |

1. Combine the ice cream, egg, grape juice, ice, and salt in a blender and blend until aerated and homogeneous.

2. Pour into four cold glasses. Top with the desired amount of seltzer water and enjoy!

# VERMONT FLUFF

THE Vermont fluff is a beverage I discovered in a delightful book titled *300 Ways to Serve Eggs*, published in 1953. As a fan of egg-based drinks, I was intrigued by this recipe because it offers a unique twist on the typical flips and nogs I usually make.

This particular recipe distinguishes itself from others by being more substantial and resembling a dessert rather than just a sweet drink. The Italian meringue, which floats on top, adds significant body to the beverage, especially when mixed in. The flavors are delightful, and I've enhanced the original recipe with grated nutmeg, cinnamon, and a pinch of salt, making it the perfect drink for a fall gathering. ✦ *Makes 2 servings*

2 large eggs, separated
1½ cups (360 mL) milk
½ cup (120 mL) maple syrup
Pinch ground cinnamon, plus more for dusting (optional)

Pinch freshly grated nutmeg, plus more for dusting (optional)
⅛ teaspoon cream of tartar
Pinch salt

1. In a mixing bowl, combine both egg yolks with 1 egg white and beat together until frothy.

2. Add the milk, ¼ cup of the maple syrup, and the cinnamon and nutmeg (if using). Pour into two glasses and place in the refrigerator to chill.

3. In a stand mixer fitted with the whisk attachment, whisk the remaining egg white and the cream of tartar on medium-high speed until you reach soft peaks, 7 to 10 minutes.

4. Meanwhile, add the remaining ¼ cup maple syrup and the salt to a small saucepan and bring to a boil. Boil the syrup for 3 minutes.

5. With the mixer on high speed, slowly pour the hot syrup into the egg white in a steady stream. The egg white will thicken and the Italian meringue will be complete.

6. Remove the chilled glasses from the refrigerator and top each drink with the maple meringue. Serve each glass with a straw or a long spoon. Garnish with a light dusting of cinnamon or freshly grated nutmeg if desired.

# The BEEF FIZZ

OVER the years that I've been sharing content through Retro Recipes, some have criticized me for making too many "safe" choices and not enough that are weird and off-putting. I disagree. In fact, I expect many of the recipes I try to turn out terribly, yet somehow they often still work!

Then the internet introduced me to the beef fizz. From my research, it seems this drink likely originated in the 1950s or '60s, during the rising popularity of lower-calorie meals. The beef fizz is less of a refreshing beverage and more like a dreadful appetizer for a dinner party, but it is technically still a drink. One that could benefit from a generous amount of alcohol, but I digress.

Let me clarify: This beverage should definitely stay in the past. I am not including it in this book for any reason other than to challenge your bravery in giving it a try, as I did.

*Laissez le bon temps rouler*—"Let the good times roll." ✦ *Makes 6 servings*

3 (10.5-ounce/298 mL) cans condensed beef broth

1 cup (240 mL) ginger ale, chilled

2 tablespoons (30 mL) fresh lemon juice

1. Combine all the ingredients and pour over ice in chilled glasses.

2. Or don't.

# SWEETS, CAKES & PIES

**WHETHER** I'm craving a rich, custardy ice cream or a tart, flaky pie, I've always had a sweet tooth—and I know I'm not alone. In fact, I venture to guess that many of you purchased this book just to see what I recommended in this chapter! There's something truly special about desserts, especially when we consider the last century of American history. From cakes bursting with butter, sugar, and eggs, like classic pound cakes, to recipes designed for families during wartime when rations were scarce, there has always been something sweet to serve at the dinner table once the main course was finished (and yes, I noticed you feeding the dog your peas).

Though we all have that friend who vocally expresses a lack of interest in sweets and prefers to finish their meals with something salty or savory, it has been well documented how much humans *love* sweets. There isn't a cookbook in my collection that isn't riddled with pastries, pies, cakes, and colorful treats for company. Historically, humanity craves sugar, but I've always been amazed with the range and variety

of ways that we express it. And depending on the decade, the recipes were simply created out of necessity, like the War Cake (page 171), which entirely lacked eggs, milk, and butter because of rationing.

Before the 1940s, the world had never been properly introduced to the chocolate chip cookie, which is now arguably America's favorite cookie. History speaks loudest to me through our sweets, because our ancestors created masterpieces from missing pieces.

Whether you're seeking something cold and creamy, warm and tart, or spongy and sweet, the wide variety of recipes included here not only please my taste buds but also ignite pleasant memories and transport me back to my childhood. As a passionate pie lover, I felt it was important to contribute some of my favorites that will hopefully bring a smile to your face. So, get ready to bake until your heart is content, and remember to close your eyes and savor every bite—you'll find it truly enhances the experience and will make you look *really serious.*

# FROZEN CUSTARD ICE CREAM

W H E N I discover a shop that specializes in not just ice cream, but *frozen custard* ice cream, there's no stopping me. Frozen custard is creamier than regular ice cream, and its richness *really* locks in more flavor, which is crucial since cold foods generally register less on our taste buds.

Frozen custard as we know it today was created in 1919 by the Kohr brothers in Coney Island, Brooklyn. They had an ice cream shop near the boardwalk and realized that adding extra egg yolks to their ice cream made it creamier on the palate and helped it stay colder. Their customers thought this was a great idea, too—reportedly, the Kohr brothers sold over eighteen thousand cones during their first weekend on the boardwalk!

Frozen custard was later popularized in the Midwest during the 1933 World's Fair in Chicago, where a vendor set up a frozen custard stand, and its popularity spread like wildfire. Today, it's still loved by millions of Midwesterners and one wildly enthusiastic South Floridian. ✦ *Makes 10 servings*

4 cups (960 mL) heavy cream
1 cup (237 mL) milk
1 teaspoon (5 g) salt

1 teaspoon (5 mL) vanilla bean paste or
    seeds scraped from 1 vanilla bean
6 large egg yolks
¾ cup (150 g) sugar

1. In a small, heavy-bottomed saucepan, combine the cream, milk, salt, and vanilla. Scald by briefly bringing to a boil, then immediately remove from the heat.

2. In a large heatproof bowl, whisk the egg yolks until frothy, gradually adding the sugar in thirds while whisking. The eggs should be pale yellow and creamy.

3. Remove a ladle of the scalded cream from the pot and pour into the egg yolk mixture, whisking constantly to prevent the yolks from scrambling. Add another ladle or two, whisking constantly, then add the rest and whisk it in.

4. Wash out the pot, pour in an inch or two of water, and bring to a boil. Set the bowl on top of the pot of boiling water and allow the custard to gently cook for about 10 minutes, whisking frequently, until it thickens.

5. If you used a vanilla bean, strain the custard. Transfer the custard to an ice cream maker. Follow the manufacturer's instructions to churn and freeze the ice cream.

6. Allow to thoroughly chill, then transfer to a freezer-safe container to serve and store.

N O T E S : *You can easily change the flavor of this ice cream by adding some chocolate or ground coffee to the cream during step 1. This will allow the fattiness of the cream to absorb the flavors and will help to melt things like chocolate or butterscotch pieces. Or you can fold in a fruit puree or cut-up fruit, nuts, or seeds toward the end of churning.*

# BRAZIL NUT CAKE

BRAZIL nuts, often the overlooked giants in your grandma's trail mix, are exceptional for their unique blend of micronutrients. They come from one of the most resilient trees in the Amazon rainforest. Around the turn of the century, Brazil nuts gained popularity in the United States due to new trade deals with South America and aggressive promotion, leading to the creation of many innovative recipes, including this delicious Brazil nut cake.

Since Brazil nuts are high in selenium—which can become toxic at excessive levels—I reduced their quantity and replaced some with the sweet flavor of macadamia nuts and the rich texture of walnuts. This combination not only enhances the cake but also makes it tastier than one made with just Brazil nuts. You'll definitely want to enjoy another slice! ✦ *Makes 8 servings*

1 cup (140 g) Brazil nuts, plus 8 whole
    nuts and additional chopped nuts
    (optional) for garnish
½ cup (60 g) macadamia nuts
½ cup (55 g) walnuts
1 cup (200 g) sugar
1 teaspoon (5 g) salt
6 large eggs, room temperature,
    separated
½ teaspoon (2 g) cream of tartar

FOR THE WHITE ICING
4 cups (460 g) confectioners' sugar
½ cup (95 g) vegetable shortening
½ cup (113 g) unsalted butter, softened
1 teaspoon (5 g) salt
2 tablespoons (30 mL) water
1 teaspoon (5 mL) vanilla bean paste

1. Preheat the oven to 325°F (160°C). Using a food processor or finely chopping by hand, process the Brazil nuts, macadamia nuts, and walnuts into an extremely fine grind, like breadcrumbs.

2. Combine the ground nuts, sugar, and salt in a large mixing bowl.

3. In another large bowl, beat the egg yolks until pale and foamy. Fold into the sugar and nut mixture. The mixture will be thick.

4. In a clean mixing bowl, whip the egg whites and cream of tartar to stiff peaks. Fold the egg whites into the nut batter.

5. Transfer the batter to a 9-inch springform cake pan. Bake for 20 minutes. Turn the oven temperature up to 375°F (190°C) and bake for 10 minutes more. Then turn the temperature back down to 325°F (160°C) for 30 minutes. This will allow the outside to brown and the inside to slowly set for a delicate crumb texture. Allow the cake to cool completely in the pan.

6. Combine all the ingredients for the white icing in a bowl and beat for several minutes with an electric mixer until thick.

7. Remove the cake from the springform pan and completely cover with icing. Garnish with Brazil nuts and serve.

# ORANGE SHERBET

HOW many of you are reading this saying "sher-bert"? If you are, fret not, as you're not alone. This bright and refreshing dessert is nothing new but has long been enjoyed, with mid-century cookbooks offering recipes that are a "sure-bet" to yield delicious results.

Sherbet actually has its lineage driving back to the twelfth century, in the Middle East, and is a cognate of the Persian word *sharbat*, which was a sweetened fruit beverage. It was common, during my research, to find in my cookbooks suggested menus for a family dinner that would include sherbet as a palate cleanser between courses, rather than simply as a dessert.

During World War II, sherbet was heavily promoted as a tasty sweet treat that could be made without cream, which was in short supply for common desserts like ice cream or custards. Whether you're a lover of a classic ice cream or crave the fruitier notes of the past, this sherbet is an easy winner for any dinner. ✦ *Makes 6 servings*

| | |
|---|---|
| 2 cups (480 mL) fresh orange juice from about 6 medium oranges | 1 cup (200 g) sugar |
| Grated zest of 1 orange | ½ cup (120 mL) heavy cream |
| | ½ cup (120 mL) milk |

1. In a large bowl, combine the orange juice, zest, and $^2/_3$ cup of the sugar. Mix until the sugar has fully dissolved.

2. In another bowl, combine the heavy cream with the remaining $^1/_3$ cup sugar and whip to stiff peaks.

3. Whisk the milk into the orange mixture, then fold in the sweetened whipped cream.

4. Chill in the refrigerator for 2 hours, then transfer to an ice cream maker. Follow the manufacturer's instructions to churn and freeze the sherbet. Serve right away for a soft-serve consistency or freeze for a firmer consistency.

# WAR CAKE

THIS cake has had many names from as early as the 1910s to the 1940s, including Depression cake, Canadian war cake, and even the clever "eggless, milkless, butterless cake." However, I insist on keeping the butter in *my* version.

During World War I, the Great Depression, and even into World War II, this cake was a source of comfort for millions of families, providing a sweet treat to help them unwind after long days of hard work. Despite its somewhat foreboding name and the hardships associated with its history, it is actually a delicious cake, packed with spices and the perfect amount of sweetness. So, if you find yourself short on perishable ingredients, give this recipe a try! ✦ *Makes 8 servings*

1¼ cups (310 mL) plus 1 tablespoon (15 mL) water
1 cup (200 g) brown sugar
⅓ cup (75 g) unsalted butter
2 cups (360 g) raisins
2 teaspoons (5 g) ground cinnamon
½ teaspoon (1 g) freshly grated nutmeg
½ teaspoon (1 g) ground cloves
1 teaspoon (5 g) baking soda
1 teaspoon (5 g) salt

2 cups (240 g) all-purpose flour, sifted
1 teaspoon (5 g) baking powder

FOR THE 7-MINUTE ICING
1 cup (200 g) sugar
½ teaspoon (2 g) cream of tartar
¼ teaspoon (1.25 g) salt
2 large egg whites, room temperature
3 tablespoons (45 mL) water
1 teaspoon (5 mL) vanilla bean paste

1. In a medium saucepan, combine 1¼ cups of the water, the brown sugar, butter, raisins, cinnamon, nutmeg, and cloves. Bring to a boil and cook for 5 minutes. Remove from the heat and set aside to cool.

2. Preheat the oven to 325°F (160°C). Butter and flour a 9-inch cake pan.

3. In a large bowl, dissolve the baking soda and salt in the remaining 1 tablespoon water. Add the cooled spice mixture, flour, and baking powder and mix well. Transfer to the prepared cake pan.

4. Bake for 50 to 60 minutes, or until a cake tester inserted in the center comes out clean. Allow to cool completely on a rack.

5. To make the icing, combine the sugar, cream of tartar, salt, egg whites, and water in a small saucepan placed over medium-low heat. Using an electric mixer, beat the mixture for 5 to 7 minutes, or until the icing is light and fluffy with stiff peaks and all of the sugar has dissolved. It should not be gritty, but have more of a marshmallow-like texture. Remove from the heat and mix in the vanilla.

6. Transfer to the icing to a piping bag or use an offset spatula to frost the cake. Cut into slices and enjoy.

# The ORIGINAL
# CHOCOLATE CHIP COOKIE

◇◇◇◇◇◇◇◇◇◇◇◇◇◇◇◇◇◇◇◇ **1930s** ◇◇◇◇◇◇◇◇◇◇◇◇◇◇◇◇◇◇◇◇

WHEN I ask people, "When do you think the chocolate chip cookie was invented?" I often hear guesses from the 1700s or 1800s. While that isn't entirely inaccurate—since cookies have been around for hundreds of years and many have included chocolate, either in melted form or as cocoa powder—it may come as a surprise to learn that the chocolate chip cookie we know today was actually created by Ruth Wakefield in 1939 at the Toll House Inn in Massachusetts.

Wakefield was already famous for her chocolate cookies, but when she ran out of cocoa powder, she decided to add a chopped chocolate bar to the batter, hoping it would melt. Instead, she stumbled upon something entirely new and delicious. ✦ *Makes 2 dozen cookies*

1 cup (225 g) unsalted butter, softened
¾ cup (150 g) brown sugar
¾ cup (150 g) granulated sugar
2 large eggs (80 g), separated
1 teaspoon (5 g) baking soda
1 teaspoon (5 g) hot water
2¼ cups (270 g) all-purpose flour, sifted

1 teaspoon (5 g) salt
1 cup (110 g) walnuts, finely chopped
1 (12-ounce/340 g) bag semisweet
    chocolate chips
1 teaspoon (5 mL) vanilla bean paste
Flaky sea salt, for sprinkling (optional)

1. In the bowl of a stand mixer fitted with the paddle attachment, cream the butter on medium-low speed until it is malleable, 3 to 5 minutes. Add the brown sugar and granulated sugar and continue to cream until pale in color, 3 to 5 minutes.

2. Weigh the egg yolks in a clean container. Slowly add the egg whites until the scale reads 80 grams. Add this mixture to the mixer bowl and mix on low speed.

3. Dissolve the baking soda in the hot water and add to the mixer. Add the flour and salt and increase the speed to medium. Add the walnuts, chocolate chips, and vanilla and mix to combine.

4. Chill the dough in the refrigerator for at least 1 hour, but preferably overnight. This will allow the flavors to blend and the butter to solidify again, allowing a better bake of the cookies.

5. When you're ready to bake, preheat the oven to 375°F (190°C). Line two rimmed baking sheets with parchment paper or silicone baking mats.

6. Using an ice cream scoop, scoop balls of dough that are a bit larger than a golf ball. Arrange them 2 inches apart on the prepared baking sheets. If desired, top each with a tiny pinch of flaky sea salt. Bake for 10 to 12 minutes, rotating the sheets halfway through. Allow to cool for a few minutes and serve.

# CHOCO-NUT TOASTIES

SOME of my favorite cookbook recipes are ones that offer inventive new ways to use traditional ingredients. Many of these recipes were inspired by cooks who had to get creative with the limited food rations available to them, and this recipe is a perfect example of that resourcefulness.

In many homes, freshly baked bread would often become a bit stale, leading folks to either discard it or find new ways to use it. In this recipe, I use my Buttermilk Bread (page 62), remove the crusts, and turn it into sweet bars that are spread with chocolate-hazelnut spread (I use Nutella) and rolled in coconut flakes. This recipe comes together quickly and makes for a delightful small bite at a party. ✦ *Makes 10 to 12 servings*

**1 loaf Buttermilk Bread (page 62) or other bread, sliced**
**¼ cup (70 g) chocolate-hazelnut spread**
**2 large eggs, beaten**
**¼ cup (60 mL) milk**

**1 teaspoon (5 g) sugar**
**½ teaspoon (1 g) ground cinnamon**
**½ teaspoon (3 g) salt**
**1 cup (70 g) sweetened coconut flakes**

1. Preheat the oven to 400°F (200°C). Line a rimmed baking sheet with aluminum foil.

2. Remove the crusts from the bread and cut the slices into 1 × 2-inch rectangles. Spread the chocolate-hazelnut spread on one side of each piece of bread, then sandwich two pieces together, forming a sandwich.

3. In a shallow dish, beat together the eggs, milk, sugar, cinnamon, and salt. Put the coconut flakes in another shallow dish. Dip each sandwich in the egg mixture to coat on all sides. Then roll and cover all sides in the coconut flakes and place on the prepared baking sheet. Bake for 10 to 15 minutes, or until toasted. Serve warm.

**NOTE:** *You can replace the chocolate-hazelnut filling with caramel or even jam.*

# PINEAPPLE UPSIDE-DOWN POKE CAKE

◇◇◇◇◇◇◇◇◇◇◇◇◇◇◇◇◇◇◇◇◇  1920s  ◇◇◇◇◇◇◇◇◇◇◇◇◇◇◇◇◇◇◇◇◇

A pineapple upside-down cake is one of the most iconic desserts in American culture. While apple pie may rival its fame, both desserts have a rich history in American cuisine. In the 1800s, upside-down cakes were made in special cast-iron pans with legs, known as "spiders," which allowed them to be cooked over an open fire. This technique inspired the name "spider cakes." The concept of an inverted dessert likely originated from the French tarte tatin.

Pineapples are a challenging fruit to grow, taking nearly two full years to mature before they can be harvested. Due to this lengthy growth period, they were considered a luxury fruit for centuries, often associated with royalty. At lavish gatherings, pineapples were used as centerpieces to showcase wealth, and some people would even rent pineapples for events if they couldn't afford to buy one.

By the turn of the century, pineapples became more widely farmed. In the 1920s, the Dole pineapple company launched a nationwide competition encouraging people to submit their best pineapple dishes, featuring Dole canned pineapple. Nearly three thousand entries for pineapple upside-down cake were received, leading the Dole company to promote the cake widely, which significantly boosted its popularity. The 1950s are often considered the peak of the pineapple upside-down cake's fame; by that time it had transitioned from a dessert reserved for special occasions to a staple recipe every housewife was expected to know how to make.

While testing this recipe, I kept asking myself what I could do with the extra butterscotch spread and pineapple juice. I felt the sponge itself was tasty but a bit dry, so I took the leftover pineapple rings that wouldn't fit in the pan and cut them up and added them to the batter, while making a pineapple-caramel glaze with the juice and butterscotch. ✦ *Makes 8 servings*

FOR THE BUTTERSCOTCH SPREAD
½ cup (113 g) unsalted butter, softened
1 cup (200 g) packed brown sugar
1 tablespoon (21 g) honey
½ teaspoon (2.5 mL) almond extract
¼ teaspoon (1.25 mL) vanilla bean paste
1 (20-ounce/567 g) can pineapple rings, drained and juice reserved
15 to 20 maraschino cherries
Kosher salt, for sprinkling

FOR THE CAKE
1½ cups (180 g) cake flour, plus more for sprinkling
2 teaspoons (10 g) baking powder
½ cup (113 g) unsalted butter, softened
¼ cup (50 g) granulated sugar
¼ cup (50 g) brown sugar
1 tablespoon (15 mL) milk
1 teaspoon (5 mL) vanilla bean paste
2 large eggs

FOR THE PINEAPPLE-CARAMEL GLAZE
1 tablespoon (14 g) unsalted butter, cold

*Recipe continues* ➤

1. Preheat the oven to 350°F (175°C).

2. To make the butterscotch spread, in the bowl of a stand mixer fitted with the paddle attachment, combine the butter, brown sugar, honey, almond extract, and vanilla. Mix on medium speed until well blended. Spread about half of the mixture on the bottom of a 9-inch cake pan. Reserve the rest in the refrigerator for the glaze. Reserve 2 pineapple rings for the cake and arrange the rest on top of the butterscotch spread, dotting the spaces between with the maraschino cherries. Sprinkle lightly with kosher salt and set side.

3. To make the cake, in a small bowl, sift together the flour and baking powder. In a large bowl, cream together the butter, granulated sugar, and brown sugar until light, fluffy, and pale in color. Add the milk and vanilla, then add the eggs, one at a time, blending fully before adding the next. Add the sifted dry ingredients in three portions and mix for several minutes, until a silky batter has formed. Finely dice the reserved pineapple rings and sprinkle about a tablespoon of cake flour on them, then fold them into the batter.

4. Pour the batter into the cake pan, on top of the pineapple rings and cherries. Bake for 20 minutes, then rotate the pan and continue to bake for another 20 to 25 minutes, or until golden brown.

5. While the cake is baking, prepare the pineapple-caramel glaze. Combine the reserved pineapple juice from the can and the reserved butterscotch spread in a small saucepan and bring to a boil. Cook, whisking constantly, until the liquid begins to thicken slightly and the bubbles lessen, 7 to 10 minutes. It shouldn't be a thick caramel, but thin and pourable. Remove from the heat and whisk in the cold butter. Poke a dozen or more holes in the surface of the cake with a skewer. Pour half of the glaze on top of the cake in the pan (which will end up being the bottom of the cake).

6. Allow the cake to cool completely. Carefully invert the cake pan onto a platter, then drizzle the remaining pineapple caramel glaze over the top of the cake. Cut, serve, and enjoy!

# BUTTERSCOTCH BREAD PUDDING

◇◇◇◇◇◇◇◇◇◇◇◇◇◇◇◇◇◇◇◇◇◇◇◇◇◇ **1930s** ◇◇◇◇◇◇◇◇◇◇◇◇◇◇◇◇◇◇◇◇◇◇◇◇◇◇

BREAD pudding has always been my go-to recipe for using up stale leftover bread. This dish has been around for centuries and was commonly regarded as a peasant's meal because it made use of stale bread. When you're a kid, it's normal to get hung up on things like leftovers, but as an adult, you learn to get creative in reducing waste and making something tasty. Bread pudding became an exciting way for me to reduce waste while enjoying an absolutely delicious treat.

Throughout the 1900s, bread pudding was considered a staple in many cookbooks, as it was essential to utilize everything you had! I believe I could open any book in my collection and find at least one recipe for the dish. While each cookbook offers its unique twist on bread pudding, I've particularly fallen in love with this version, which I serve with a hot, silky butterscotch sauce, perfectly complementing the custardy pudding. ✦ *Makes 10 servings*

### FOR THE BUTTERSCOTCH
1 cup (200 g) packed brown sugar
½ cup (120 mL) light corn syrup
3 tablespoons (42 g) unsalted butter
1 teaspoon (5 g) salt
½ cup (120 mL) heavy cream

### FOR THE PUDDING
1 loaf day-old bread, cut into cubes
½ cup (113 g) unsalted butter, melted
2 tablespoons (24 g) plus 1½ cups (300 g)
   granulated sugar

4 large eggs plus 2 large egg yolks
4 cups (480 mL) heavy cream
1 tablespoon (15 g) kosher salt
2 teaspoons (10 mL) vanilla bean paste
2 cups (240 g) pecans, crushed (optional)

### FOR THE SALTED WHIPPED CREAM
1 cup (240 mL) heavy cream, chilled
¼ cup (30 g) confectioners' sugar
1 teaspoon (5 g) salt
½ teaspoon (2.5 mL) vanilla bean paste

1. To make the butterscotch, in a medium saucepan, combine the brown sugar, corn syrup, butter, and salt and bring to a boil over medium heat. Whisk constantly and boil for 3 to 5 minutes, until syrupy. Remove from the heat. Add the heavy cream and stir until smooth. Refrigerate until needed.

2. To make the pudding, in a large bowl, toss the cubes of bread with the melted butter and 2 tablespoons of the granulated sugar. In another bowl, beat the eggs and egg yolks with the remaining 1½ cups sugar until they are pale yellow and fluffy. Add the heavy cream, salt, and vanilla to the egg mixture. Pour the liquid over the cubed bread and add the crushed pecans, if using.

3. Transfer the bread custard to a 9 × 13-inch glass baking dish and spread out evenly. Cover with plastic wrap and refrigerate for at least 2 hours, or overnight for best results.

4. Preheat the oven to 325°F (160°C).

*Recipe continues* ➤

5. Unwrap the casserole dish and bake for about $1\frac{1}{2}$ hours, or until the top is golden brown and a cake tester inserted in the middle comes out clean. Allow to cool for 10 minutes before serving. Meanwhile, warm the butterscotch sauce.

6. To make the salted whipped cream, in a medium bowl, add the cold heavy cream and beat with a whisk until bubbly. Add the confectioners' sugar, salt, and vanilla and continue to whip until you can scoop a dollop with a spoon and it holds its shape. Be careful not to whip too much, or you could overchurn the cream and cause it to break.

7. Serve the bread pudding topped with the butterscotch sauce and a nice dollop of the salted whipped cream.

# MARDI GRAS PARTY CAKE

◇◇◇◇◇◇◇◇◇◇◇◇◇◇◇◇◇◇◇◇◇◇◇◇   1950s   ◇◇◇◇◇◇◇◇◇◇◇◇◇◇◇◇◇◇◇◇◇◇◇◇

**THIS** incredible cake was created by Eunice Surles in Louisiana and won the grand prize award of $25,000 in 1959's Pillsbury Bake-Off. I came across this tasty treat while filming my series on award-winning recipes from vintage contests and fell in love with the rich butterscotch taste, the wonderful texture, and the airy sponge. This cake is a labor of love but not difficult to create, so simply follow the steps and hum some songs of the bayou because you're about to be transported to Bourbon Street! ✦ *Makes 8 servings*

### FOR THE CAKE
⅔ cup (160 g) butterscotch morsels
¼ cup (60 mL) water
2¼ cups (270 g) all-purpose flour, sifted
1¼ cup (250 g) granulated sugar
1 teaspoon (5 g) salt
1 teaspoon (5 g) baking soda
½ teaspoon (2.5 g) baking powder
½ cup (113 g) unsalted butter, softened
3 large eggs
1 cup (240 mL) buttermilk

### FOR THE FILLING
½ cup (100 g) granulated sugar
1 tablespoon (8 g) cornstarch
½ cup (120 mL) evaporated milk or
    half-and-half
⅓ cup (80 mL) water
⅓ cup (80 g) butterscotch morsels
1 large egg yolk
2 tablespoons (28 g) unsalted butter
1 cup (70 g) sweetened coconut flakes
1 cup (120 g) chopped walnuts

### FOR THE SEA FOAM ICING
2 large egg whites, room
    temperature
1½ cups (300 g) brown sugar
5 tablespoons (75 mL) cold water
1 teaspoon (5 mL) vanilla bean paste

1. Preheat the oven to 350°F (175°C). Generously butter and flour two 9-inch round cake pans and line the bottoms with parchment paper.

2. To make the cake, combine the butterscotch morsels and the water in a small saucepan, and cook over medium heat, stirring until melted and smooth. Set aside to cool.

3. In a stand mixer fitted with the paddle attachment, combine the flour, sugar, salt, baking soda, baking powder, butter, eggs, buttermilk, and cooled butterscotch mixture. Mix on low speed until moistened, then mix on medium speed for 3 to 5 minutes to fully blend.

4. Divide the batter evenly between the two prepared cake pans and bake for 20 to 30 minutes, or until a cake tester inserted in the center comes out clean. Cool for 7 to 10 minutes in the pans, remove from the pans, and allow to cool completely on a wire rack.

*Recipe continues* ➤

5. To make the filling, combine the granulated sugar, cornstarch, evaporated milk, water, butter-scotch morsels, and egg yolk in a medium saucepan. Cook over medium heat, stirring constantly, until the mixture thickens, 5 to 7 minutes, then remove from the heat. Mix in the butter, coconut, and walnuts and allow to cool slightly.

6. To make the icing, pour an inch or two of water into a medium saucepan and bring to a boil. Combine all of the icing ingredients in a heatproof bowl and place on top of the pot of boiling water. Whisk constantly by hand or using an electric mixer for about 7 minutes, until the icing is thick and the sugar has completely dissolved.

7. To assemble the cake, place one of the cooled cake layers on a serving plate, top-side down. Spread half of the coconut filling on it and top with the second cake, top-side up. Spread the remaining coconut filling in the center of the top and expand outward, leaving an inch around the border uncovered. Frost the sides of the cake with the icing and cover over the edges that were left exposed. Allow to set in the refrigerator for at least 1 hour before cutting.

# LIGHTNING CAKE

◇◇◇◇◇◇◇◇◇◇◇◇◇◇◇◇◇◇◇◇◇◇◇  **1 8 9 0 s**  ◇◇◇◇◇◇◇◇◇◇◇◇◇◇◇◇◇◇◇◇◇◇◇

T H E lightning cake was an incredibly popular dessert that was commonly made when unexpected guests would arrive. Believed to come from the German *Blitzkuchen*, meaning lightning cake, it was first mentioned in cookbooks in the 1800s, eventually finding its way to American cookbooks in the 1940s. The cake was most popular during the 1960s, after it was published in a Betty Crocker cookbook as "blitz torte."

I have seen variations that use the egg whites to make a meringue that would cover the top, but the version I fell in love with was from *The Fannie Farmer Cookbook*, which offered the delicious "lazy daisy" topping of butterscotch and coconut. Not only is this a quick and easy one-bowl recipe, but the flavors make this cake so good that it disappears faster than a flash of lightning.

✦ *Makes 8 servings*

### FOR THE CAKE
2 large eggs
1 teaspoon (5 mL) vanilla bean paste
1 cup (200 g) granulated sugar
1 cup (120 g) cake flour
1 teaspoon (4 g) baking powder
½ teaspoon (2.5 g) salt
½ cup (120 mL) milk
1 tablespoon (14 g) unsalted butter

### FOR THE TOPPING
3 tablespoons (42 g) unsalted butter, melted
3 tablespoons (36 g) brown sugar
2 tablespoons (30 mL) heavy cream
½ cup (35 g) sweetened coconut flakes

1. Preheat the oven to 375°F (190°C). Butter and flour a 9-inch springform pan.

2. In a large bowl, whisk together the eggs and vanilla, adding the sugar in four portions and whisking after each addition until fully incorporated.

3. In a medium bowl, sift together the cake flour, baking powder, and salt.

4. In a small saucepan, heat the milk and butter over low heat just until the butter is melted and the mixture is hot; do not let it boil.

5. Pour the dry ingredients into the egg mixture, then pour in the hot milk mixture. Mix well. Pour the batter into the prepared baking pan. Bake for 20 to 25 minutes, or until a cake tester inserted in the middle comes out clean. Allow the cake to cool for 10 minutes. Turn on the broiler.

6. Combine all the topping ingredients in a small bowl and mix well. Spread the topping on top of the cake and place under the broiler for 3 to 5 minutes to caramelize the sugars, rotating the pan every minute or so to make sure it browns evenly and doesn't burn.

7. Allow the cake to cool completely before releasing the springform and removing the cake from the pan.

# GELATIN RAINBOW CAKE

I first discovered this cake in *Joys of Jell-O*, published in 1961, and knew it would be an essential addition to the book. There is something so quintessential about a gelatin-based dessert, and this colorful cake is so much fun to share with others.

This particular recipe took some testing, as many old cookbooks lack the technical tricks needed for success, so please thoroughly read through before trying to make this. Trust me, you don't want to spend hours making this to have it fall apart or not set properly. It requires quite a bit of patience, planning, and perhaps practice, but it will be sure to spark joy to anyone that receives a slice. You'll need to have everything ready to go, since timing is essential for this to work. You will need five bowls or plastic deli containers that you can use to keep each gelatin flavor separate. ✦ *Makes 12 servings*

### FOR THE CAKE
5 (3-ounce/85 g) packages gelatin mix, in different flavors such as black cherry, lime, lemon, orange, and strawberry
7½ cups (1.75 L) water

### FOR THE ICING
1½ cups (360 mL) heavy cream
½ cup (60 g) confectioners' sugar
1 teaspoon (5 g) vanilla bean paste
½ teaspoon (2.5 g) salt

1. Line a 9-inch springform pan or mold with a double layer of wax paper, leaving about 3 inches of overhang on each end.

2. In a small saucepan, bring 1 cup water to a rapid boil. Add one of the packages of gelatin mix and whisk constantly for about 2 minutes or until completely dissolved. If the gelatin mixture begins to rise, remove the pot from the heat for a moment and allow the gelatin mixture to lower and settle again before continuing to boil. This will prevent the mixture from boiling over. Once the gelatin is dissolved, transfer the mixture to a bowl and add ½ cup cold water. Rinse out the pot and repeat the process to make the other gelatin flavors, using a different bowl for each.

3. Fill a large metal bowl halfway with crushed ice, then place another metal bowl on top of the ice. Pour the first flavor of gelatin into the top metal bowl and begin to whisk. After about 2 minutes, you will notice it begins to bubble a bit more, with some liquid still on the bottom. Continue to whisk until the gelatin base has doubled in volume and any liquid has disappeared and become foamy, 3 to 5 minutes. When you can easily scoop a large dollop of the gelatin, like scooping a stiff meringue, spoon the gelatin into the prepared springform pan and use the bottom of the spoon or an offset spatula to level off the surface. Place the springform pan in the refrigerator for 5 to 7 minutes, until the next layer is ready to be added.

*Recipe continues* ➤

4. Rinse out the metal bowl and repeat with the remaining gelatin flavors in the order listed for a rainbow effect. Generally, by the time the next layer is ready, the previous layer should be set enough to carefully spoon on top of. Once all the layers are complete, allow the cake to set in the refrigerator to fully firm up for at least 6 hours, or overnight.

5. To make the icing, combine the cream, confectioner's sugar, vanilla, and salt in a medium bowl and whip with a whisk until you have a rich whipped cream topping. Remove the cake from the springform pan to a serving platter. Frost the cake with the icing and serve.

**NOTES:** *The gelatin is extremely prone to staining clothing or countertops, so work with caution and keep some cleaner handy.*

*I have found it more effective to add the gelatin to the boiling water in the pot and continue to cook, rather than simply pour boiling water from a kettle into the bowl with the gelatin. I also found it is much easier to control the proper texture by hand whisking, rather than using an electric mixer. This will prevent too much aeration, and you can also feel the proper consistency from the natural resistance while it's setting in the ice bath.*

*I recommend using a large spoon to transfer the gelatin to the springform pan, not pouring the layers onto each other. There's more control and less risk of disturbing the layers.*

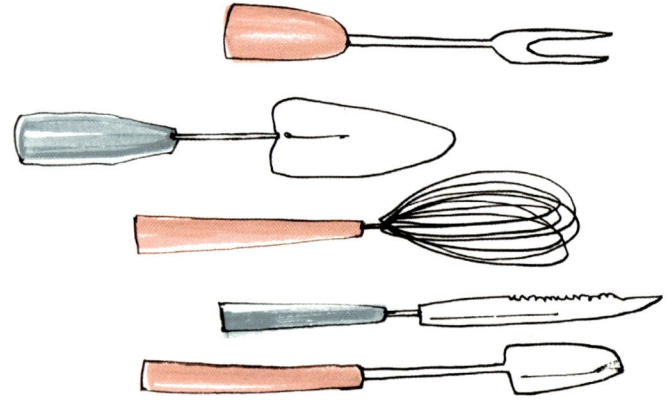

# DEVIL SQUARES

THIS recipe is an accidental copycat of my favorite childhood junk food—Little Debbie's Devil Squares. They are perfect in every way, but will sadly disappear much faster than the time it takes to make them.

At the end of the 1800s, the angel's food cake was created, gaining its namesake from the airy, light sponge that was made from utilizing egg whites as the leavening agent, rather than baking powder or soda. So, naturally, around the turn of the twentieth century, its more indulgent, decadent counterpart, devil's food cake, was created.

Devil's food cake deviated from traditional chocolate cakes in its use of cocoa powder rather than melted chocolate, which gave it the trademark darker color and deeper cocoa flavor. It also utilized sour milk, or buttermilk, rather than the more common milk or cream. This made it one of the most popular recipes during World War II, when rations of chocolate and cream were incredibly difficult to acquire. When your delivery of milk was beginning to turn and sour, this recipe was the perfect way to prevent waste.

In 1972, the Little Debbie company released their Devil Squares on the market and to this day, I still love them—maybe even more than when I was a kid. ✦ *Makes 24 servings*

### FOR THE CAKE
1½ cups (180 g) cake flour
6 tablespoons (42 g) cocoa powder
1 teaspoon (5 g) baking soda
½ teaspoon (2.5 g) salt
4 tablespoons (56 g) unsalted butter, softened
1 cup (200 g) sugar
1 large egg
1 cup (240 mL) buttermilk
1 teaspoon (5 mL) vanilla bean paste

### FOR THE 7-MINUTE ICING
1 cup (200 g) sugar
¼ teaspoon (1.25 g) salt
½ teaspoon (2 g) cream of tartar
2 large egg whites, room temperature
3 tablespoons (45 mL) water
1 teaspoon (5 mL) vanilla bean paste

### FOR THE CHOCOLATE GANACHE
1 cup (240 mL) heavy cream
8 ounces (227 g) semisweet chocolate bars, finely grated

1. Preheat the oven to 350°F (175°C). Butter and flour a 9 × 13-inch baking pan.

2. Sift together the flour, cocoa, baking soda, and salt three times over a sheet of parchment paper or a medium bowl.

3. Using a stand mixer or by hand, cream the softened butter, adding the sugar in four portions, until fluffy and pale in color. Add the egg and continue to beat until blended.

*Recipe continues* ➤

4. Add the dry ingredients and buttermilk to the creamed mixture in three portions each, alternating between the two and beating together after each addition until smooth. Add the vanilla. Pour the batter into the prepared cake pan. Bake until a cake tester inserted in the middle comes out clean, about 20 minutes. Allow the cake to cool completely in the pan.

5. To make the icing, combine the sugar, salt, cream of tartar, egg whites, and water in a small saucepan placed over medium-low heat. Using an electric mixer, beat the mixture for 5 to 7 minutes, or until the icing is light and fluffy with stiff peaks and all of the sugar has dissolved. It should not be gritty, but have more of a marshmallow-like texture. Remove from the heat and mix in the vanilla. Transfer to a piping bag.

6. When the cake is cool enough to handle, carefully cut it into 2-inch squares. Cut a square in half, pipe some icing onto the bottom half, and top with the other half. Set the sandwiched square on a wire rack set over a baking sheet. Repeat with the remaining squares.

7. To make the ganache, warm the cream in a small saucepan until it begins to simmer, but not boil. Put the chocolate in a small bowl and pour the warm cream over the chocolate. Allow it to sit for a couple minutes to help melt the chocolate, then whisk until it begins to thicken.

8. Pour the ganache over the devil squares on the wire rack and use an offset spatula or butter knife to spread evenly. Allow to cool completely before serving.

# PINK COCONUT LAYER CAKE

◇◇◇◇◇◇◇◇◇◇◇◇◇◇◇◇◇◇◇◇◇◇◇◇  **1950s**  ◇◇◇◇◇◇◇◇◇◇◇◇◇◇◇◇◇◇◇◇◇◇◇◇

COCONUT in a cake has always made sense to me. It's a sweet, tropical taste that works nicely with buttery, sugary ingredients and offers a wonderful texture and chew to anything it's added to. Coconut has been a popular ingredient in American cooking since Colonial times, and one of the most popular cakes to use the ingredient is the coconut layer cake.

This simple cake would often be dressed up with bright, colorful food coloring. It's pink because *everything* in the 1950s and '60s was more colorful and brighter and had more thought put into the design. If you've followed my career long enough, you know I'm a *big* fan of anything pink. So, I had to include this delicious and adorable cake in the book. ✦ *Makes 4 to 6 servings*

**FOR THE CAKE**
2 cups (240 g) cake flour, sifted
2 teaspoons (10 g) baking powder
1 teaspoon (5 g) salt
⅔ cup (150 g) unsalted butter, softened
1½ cups (300 g) sugar
3 large eggs (150 g)
⅔ cup (157 mL) whole milk
1 teaspoon (5 g) vanilla bean paste

**FOR THE 7-MINUTE ICING**
2 large egg whites (68 g), room
    temperature
1½ cups (300 g) sugar
5 tablespoons (75 mL) cold water
1½ teaspoons (7 g) light corn syrup
1 teaspoon (5 g) vanilla bean paste
Pink or red food coloring
2 cups (140 g) sweetened coconut flakes

1. Preheat the oven to 375°F (190°C). Butter and flour two 9-inch round cake pans.

2. Sift together the cake flour, baking powder, and salt three times over a sheet of parchment paper or a medium bowl.

3. In a large bowl, combine the butter and sugar and cream together until light and fluffy. In a small bowl, beat the eggs until pale yellow and light, then add to the creamed butter and sugar mixture.

4. Add the dry ingredients and milk to the creamed mixture in three portions each, alternating between the two and beating together after each addition until smooth. Mix in the vanilla. Divide the batter between the prepared cake pans and bake for 20 to 25 minutes, or until a cake tester inserted in the middle comes out clean. Let cool completely.

5. To make the icing, pour an inch or two of water into a medium saucepan and bring to a boil. Combine the egg whites, sugar, cold water, and corn syrup in a heatproof bowl and place on top of the pot of boiling water. Whisk constantly by hand or using an electric mixer for about 7 minutes, until the icing is thick and the sugar has completely dissolved. Remove the bowl and add the vanilla and then the food coloring, one drop at a time, mixing until you reach the desired shade.

6. Turn the cake out of the pans. Place one cake layer on a cake plate and frost with a generous portion of icing. Add the second layer on top and cover the entire cake with the remaining icing. Cover the cake with the coconut and serve.

# BANANA CRUNCH CAKE

THOUGH I'm a nondenominational lover of desserts with a crippling sweet tooth, over the last decade or so, I've identified less as a "cake guy"—until this banana crunch cake came along.

Created by Bonnie Brooks in 1973, this recipe won the $50,000 Grand Prize in the Pillsbury Bake-Off for the year. The recipe is incredibly simple but truly required no changes—this is as good as it gets. No fancy icing, no dusting of confectioners' sugar. It's just a damn good cake. I debated the inclusion of packaged yellow cake mix (with pudding powder included, or "super moist" on the label), since I carefully put my own spin on every other recipe in this book. But I know a good recipe when I see one, and I don't think I'd do Bonnie Brooks any favors if I deviated from her simple, perfect plan.

So, if you'd prefer to use your own cake recipe and not a box mix for this recipe, help yourself. But I promise that this recipe is so good, you won't need to. ✦ *Makes 8 servings*

½ cup (60 g) all-purpose flour
1 cup (70 g) sweetened coconut flakes
1 cup (85 g) rolled oats
¾ cup (150 g) brown sugar, firmly packed
½ cup (65 g) pecans, chopped
½ cup (113 g) unsalted butter, cut into
   small pieces

2 large very ripe bananas
½ cup (120 mL) sour cream
4 large eggs
1 (15.25-ounce/432 g) package "super
   moist" yellow cake mix (with pudding
   included)

1. Preheat the oven to 350°F (175°C). Grease and flour a 10- to 12-cup Bundt or tube pan.

2. In a food processor, combine the flour, coconut, rolled oats, brown sugar, and pecans. Pulse 10 to 15 times to blend, then cut the butter into the flour so that the mixture is crumbly.

3. In a large bowl, combine the bananas, sour cream, and eggs, mashing and blending until smooth. Add the cake mix to the banana mixture and beat together until thoroughly combined.

4. Spread one-third of the batter in the prepared pan. Sprinkle one-third of the coconut mixture on top, and repeat this process of layering until you're out of batter and crumble.

5. Bake for 50 to 60 minutes, or until a cake tester inserted in the middle comes out clean. Allow to cool for 15 minutes, then remove from the pan. Allow the cake to cool completely before serving.

# VINEGAR PIE

PIES have long served the world as a sweet or savory vessel to fill our bellies with unique or exotic ingredients. I've seen some wild pies that called for sweetbreads (the tender, delicious thymus gland of a calf), and others that are literally called "water pies." So, when I thumbed through one of my hundreds of cookbooks and found the vinegar pie, I was intrigued—but I wasn't prepared for how absolutely delicious it was.

Though the title might sound like it would sting your nostrils, sugar and vinegar are a classic combination that is essential for any sweet-and-sour flavor profile. In French cuisine, the *gastrique* is a classic sauce that helps cut through fattier proteins like duck, and similar sauce styles are found in Italian cooking with their *agrodolce*, or in Asian cookery as well with Indian chutneys and so on. When the balance is met, the flavor dances on your palate. I like to top this pie with freshly made whipped cream or a dusting of confectioners' sugar. ✦ *Makes 8 servings*

**FOR THE PIE CRUST**
1 cup (120 g) all-purpose flour
⅓ cup (40 g) cake flour
½ teaspoon (2.5 g) salt
2 tablespoons (25 g) sugar
½ cup (113 g) unsalted butter, frozen and grated
3 tablespoons (42 g) vegetable shortening, chilled
5 to 6 tablespoons (75–90 mL) ice water

**FOR THE FILLING**
4 large eggs plus 1 large egg yolk, beaten
1½ cups (250 g) sugar
¼ cup (60 g) butter, melted and cooled
1½ tablespoons apple cider vinegar
1 teaspoon (5 mL) vanilla bean paste

1. Preheat the oven to 450°F (230°C).

2. To make the pie crust, sift together the all-purpose flour, cake flour, and salt into a food processor, then add the sugar, butter, and shortening. Pulse several times while slowly drizzling in the water through the feed tube until the dough just begins to form a ball. Transfer to a bowl and refrigerate for 30 minutes to hydrate the dough and chill the butter.

3. Roll the dough out to about ¼-inch thickness. Place the dough in a 9-inch pie pan, pressing it gently into the corners. Prick the base of the pie crust several times with a fork and bake until golden brown, 10 to 12 minutes. Set aside to cool. Turn the oven temperature down to 350°F (175°C).

4. To make the filling, in a large bowl, combine the eggs and egg yolk, sugar, melted butter, vinegar, and vanilla and mix well. Pour into the cooled pie shell and bake for 40 to 50 minutes, or until the custard base is golden brown and has a slight wobble; it should reach an internal temperature of 170°F (75°C).

5. Allow to cool completely, then slice and serve.

# BUTTERMILK PIE

THIS recipe is dedicated to Fa'Tyma Pope, a long-time supporter who passed away from a rare cancer in the fall of 2024. She was a passionate chef, published author, and artist. The day before she passed away, she expressed her gratitude for our conversations about our favorite foods and celebrity chefs. I asked her if there were any recipes I could make in her memory, and she suggested buttermilk pie, which was a perfect choice. It's bright, acidic, and sweet, making it one of those dishes you can savor. I like to serve it with a dusting of confectioners' sugar or some ground cinnamon.

Buttermilk pie is often referred to as a "desperation pie," made from simple pantry ingredients. Unlike other popular pies filled with fruits or elaborate fillings, buttermilk pie was created as a practical solution, allowing thrifty home cooks to prepare something tasty and economical for their families. This pie was particularly popular during wartime when rations were scarce, providing a perfect way to use up milk that was beginning to sour.  ✦ *Makes 8 servings*

### FOR THE PIE CRUST
1 cup (120 g) all-purpose flour
⅓ cup (40 g) cake flour
½ teaspoon (2.5 g) salt
2 tablespoons (25 g) sugar
½ cup (113 g) unsalted butter, frozen
    and grated
3 tablespoons (42 g) vegetable
    shortening, chilled
5 to 6 tablespoons (75–90 mL) ice water

### FOR THE FILLING
½ cup (113 g) unsalted butter, softened
1½ cups (300 g) sugar
3 tablespoons (24 g) all-purpose flour
¼ teaspoon (1.25 g) kosher salt
3 large eggs
1 teaspoon (5 mL) vanilla bean paste
⅛ teaspoon (0.3 g) freshly grated
    nutmeg
Grated zest and juice of 1 lemon
1 cup (240 mL) buttermilk

1. Preheat the oven to 450°F (230°C).

2. To make the pie crust, sift together the all-purpose flour, cake flour, and salt into a food processor, then add the sugar, butter, and shortening. Pulse several times while slowly drizzling in the cold water through the feed tube until the dough just begins to form a ball. Transfer to a bowl and refrigerate for 30 minutes to hydrate the dough and chill the butter.

3. Roll the dough out to about ¼-inch thickness. Place the dough in a 9-inch pie pan, pressing it gently into the corners. Prick the base of the pie crust several times with a fork and bake until golden brown, 10 to 12 minutes. Set aside to cool. Turn the oven temperature down to 350°F (175°C).

4. To make the filling, cream together the softened butter and sugar in a large bowl. Mix in the flour and salt. Add the eggs, one at a time, beating until incorporated. Add the vanilla, nutmeg, lemon zest and juice, and buttermilk and mix well. Pour the filling into the cooled pie shell and bake for 35 to 40 minutes, or until set but still a little wobbly. Allow to cool completely, then slice and serve.

# DELMONICO PIE

THE Delmonico pie is truly a masterclass in simplicity. To this day, I have only found this recipe printed *once* in a book titled *Uneeda Bakers Book of Menu Magic* from 1933, and I've never found out where the recipe name came from. It has nothing to do with the famed steakhouse, to the best of my research, and yet it absolutely would hold its own next to a $200 steak dinner.

This simple pie is based around macerated strawberries and bananas with a graham cracker crust and some whipped cream. I've adjusted the recipe a wee bit just to balance flavors more and offer a pop of salinity in the whipped cream, which really elevates the flavor of everything.  ✦ *Makes 8 servings*

### FOR THE PIE CRUST
1¼ cups (140 g) graham cracker crumbs
⅓ cup (75 g) unsalted butter, melted
¼ cup (50 g) granulated sugar
⅛ teaspoon (0.6 g) salt

### FOR THE FILLING
1 cup (150 g) fresh strawberries, hulled and
    halved, plus more for garnish (optional)
1 cup (120 g) sliced ripe bananas, plus
    more for garnish (optional)
1 tablespoon (12 g) granulated sugar

### FOR THE SALTED WHIPPED CREAM
1 cup (240 mL) heavy cream
3 tablespoons (36 g) confectioners' sugar
1 teaspoon (5 mL) vanilla bean paste
1 teaspoon (5 g) salt

1. Preheat the oven to 400°F (200°C).

2. To make the pie crust, in a medium bowl, combine the graham cracker crumbs, melted butter, granulated sugar, and salt and mix well. Transfer the mixture to a 9-inch pie pan and firmly pack the crumbs into the bottom and sides using the bottom of a measuring cup. Bake for 5 to 7 minutes, or until golden brown and toasty. Allow to cool completely.

3. To make the filling, in a large bowl, combine the strawberries, bananas, and granulated sugar. Gently toss, then set aside to macerate for 10 minutes. When the graham cracker crust is cool, transfer the fruit to the pie shell and spread out evenly.

4. To make the salted whipped cream, in a medium bowl, combine the heavy cream, confectioners' sugar, vanilla, and salt. Whip to stiff peaks with a whisk by hand to ensure you don't overwhip, 1 to 2 minutes. Transfer to a piping bag fitted with a large pastry tip.

5. Top the fruit with the salted whipped cream and garnish with more strawberries and banana slices if desired.

# "OPEN SESAME" PIE

THIS recipe comes from the 1954 edition of the Pillsbury Bake-Off contest, where it won the Grand Prize for Dorothy Koteen of Washington, DC. Not only was it a massive hit at the judges' table, but it also caused a nationwide frenzy, leading to a shortage of sesame seeds almost immediately after it was published. Supermarkets across the United States were cleaned out, and it became common practice to ensure that sesame seeds were regularly restocked on the shelves.

This pie has always stuck with me because of its unique and exciting flavors. It's incredibly simple, yet the combination of toasted sesame seeds with a creamy date and vanilla filling ignites every neuron in my brain.  ✦ *Makes 8 servings*

### FOR THE PIE CRUST

**3 tablespoons (27 g) sesame seeds**
**1 cup (120 g) all-purpose flour, sifted**
**½ teaspoon (2.5 g) salt**
**⅓ cup (75 g) unsalted butter, frozen and grated**
**3 tablespoons (45 mL) cold water**

### FOR THE DATE CHIFFON FILLING

**1 (¼-ounce/42 g) packet unflavored gelatin**
**¼ cup (60 mL) cold water**
**1 cup (240 mL) milk**
**2 large egg yolks**
**¼ cup plus 2 tablespoons (75 g) sugar**
**½ teaspoon (2.5 g) salt**
**1 teaspoon (5 mL) vanilla bean paste**
**1 cup (150 g) pitted dates, chopped**
**¾ cup (180 mL) heavy cream**
**2 large egg whites, room temperature**
**2 tablespoons (25 g) sugar**
**Freshly grated nutmeg, for dusting**

1. Preheat the oven to 450°F (230°C).

2. To make the pie crust, toast the sesame seeds in a small pan over medium heat, tossing occasionally to ensure even cooking, 3 to 5 minutes. Set aside to cool.

3. Sift together the flour and salt into a food processor, then add the butter. Pulse several times while slowly drizzling in the cold water through the feed tube until the dough just begins to form a ball. Transfer to a bowl and refrigerate for 30 minutes to hydrate the dough and chill the butter.

4. Roll the dough out to about ¼-inch thickness. Sprinkle the sesame seeds over the surface of the rolled dough and gently press in with one more pass of the rolling pin. Invert the dough in a 9-inch pie pan so the sesame seeds are facing the outside. Prick the base of the pie crust several times with a fork and bake until golden brown, 10 to 12 minutes. Set aside to cool.

*Recipe continues*  ➤

5. To make the filling, in a small bowl, dissolve the gelatin in the cold water and allow to bloom for several minutes.

6. Pour an inch or two of water into a medium saucepan and bring to a boil. In a heatproof bowl, combine the milk, egg yolks, ¼ cup of the sugar, and the salt. Place the bowl on top of the pot of boiling water and whisk constantly until the mixture begins to thicken and can coat the back of a spoon. Stir in the bloomed gelatin and vanilla. Remove from the heat. Dip the chopped dates in cool water and add them to the bowl. Mix to incorporate. Allow to cool completely.

7. Whisk the egg whites to stiff peaks with the remaining 2 tablespoons sugar and fold into the date mixture. Spoon the filling into the pie shell and refrigerate for at least 1 hour to set. Dust lightly with freshly grated nutmeg just before serving.

# KEY LIME PIE

AS a Florida native, I must include one of the most celebrated desserts in American history: key lime pie. Not only is it one of my favorite pies, but it's also one of the simplest to make. Traditionally, the base consists of key lime juice, condensed milk, and eggs. In my version, I elevate the classic recipe by using cooking techniques that allow for more control, specifically by making a delicious lime curd. Additionally, I prefer to use Italian meringue instead of the traditional French meringue for its marshmallow-like texture, especially when toasted with a brûlée torch.

The history of key lime pie is quite mysterious, with several theories about its origins. One story is that it was created by coastal sponge fishermen who would snack on stale bread, condensed milk, and lime juice. Another theory posits that a private chef invented it for a wealthy client in the mid-1800s. The most compelling theory I've come across is that it was developed in the 1930s by the Borden brand, known for their sweetened condensed milk. They had already created a recipe for "magic lemon cream pie," discovering that when lemon juice was combined with egg yolks and their sweetened condensed milk, it would curdle and set without the need for heat. They later tested this method using lime juice, and the rest is history.

As someone who is quite particular about my key lime pie, I can confidently say that this version is my favorite. Though it requires more effort than what my grandmother used to put in, it will surely become your go-to recipe. ✦ *Makes 8 servings*

### FOR THE CRUST
1½ (170 g) cups graham cracker crumbs
2 tablespoons (25 g) granulated sugar
1 tablespoon (12 g) brown sugar
⅛ teaspoon (0.6 g) salt
7 tablespoons (100 g) unsalted butter, melted

### FOR THE FILLING
3 tablespoons (25 g) cornstarch
2 tablespoons (15 mL) water
1 cup (240 mL) fresh key lime juice or regular lime juice
6 large eggs plus 6 large egg yolks, beaten

1 cup (200 g) granulated sugar
¼ cup (50 g) brown sugar
½ cup (113 g) unsalted butter, cold

### FOR THE ITALIAN MERINGUE
1 cup (200 g) granulated sugar
½ cup (120 mL) water
4 large egg whites, room temperature
½ teaspoon (2 g) cream of tartar
Juice of 1 lemon (2–3 tablespoons)
Pinch salt
Grated lime zest and thinly sliced limes, for garnish (optional)

*Recipe continues*  ➤

1. Preheat the oven to 350°F (175°C).

2. To make the crust, in a large bowl, combine the graham cracker crumbs, granulated sugar, brown sugar, salt, and melted butter and mix well. Transfer the mixture to a 9-inch pie pan and firmly pack the crumbs into the bottom and sides using the bottom of a measuring cup. Bake for 10 minutes, then allow to cool completely.

3. To make the filling, pour an inch or two of water into a medium saucepan and bring to a boil. In a heatproof bowl, whisk together the cornstarch and water to make a slurry. Add the lime juice, eggs, egg yolks, granulated sugar, and brown sugar and mix well. Place the bowl on top of the pot of boiling water and continue to cook until the custard reaches about 170°F (75°C) and is thick enough to coat the back of a spoon. Remove from the heat and gradually incorporate the cold butter, whisking after each addition to emulsify the lime curd. Allow to cool.

4. To make the Italian meringue, combine the sugar and water in a small saucepan and cook over medium-high heat until it reaches the "soft ball" stage, 240°F (116°C), 10 to 15 minutes. While that is cooking, add the egg whites, cream of tartar, lemon juice, and salt to a stand mixer fitted with the whisk attachment. Whisk on high speed until medium peaks form, then slowly pour in the hot syrup while it is running, until you get the desired stiffness and the bottom of the bowl is cool to the touch. Transfer the Italian meringue to a piping bag fitted with a large pastry tip.

5. Add the lime curd to the cooled graham cracker crust, evenly spreading with an offset spatula. Top the pie with the Italian meringue. To brown the meringue, either slip the pie under the broiler for several minutes or carefully use a brûlée torch.

6. I prefer to freeze the pie and serve it cold. Alternatively, you can allow the pie to chill in the refrigerator for an hour, or until set. Grate some lime zest over the top, garnish with the lime slices if desired, and serve.

**NOTE:** *I like to add a small pinch of flaky salt on top as well. Each bite plays on your palate, offering a sweet, salty, and sour experience, which is way more fun.*

# HOLIDAY BAVARIAN PIE

1950s

THE holidays are the perfect time to showcase impressive desserts, and this recipe fits the bill. Though there isn't any direct connection between Bavarian pies and the holidays, this particular recipe (found originally in *The Good Housekeeping Christmas Cookbook* from 1958) is adapted to blend wonderful wintertime spices to perk up your palate. It features a complex yet balanced combination of flavors that keeps you coming back for more! The addition of freshly grated nutmeg adds a wonderful spice that complements the toasted coconut and whipped cream. Plus, the use of gelatin ensures a perfectly set pie that is nearly impossible to mess up.

Bavarian cream has been around in various forms since its creation in Bavaria during the seventeenth century. It was later refined by the French pastry chef Marie-Antoine Carême, who utilized gelatin to stabilize the custard for a firmer set. Traditionally, Bavarian cream was served with fruit and enjoyed as a custard dish. However, it eventually found its way into pies, giving rise to the Bavarian cream pie. This dessert gained popularity in the mid-twentieth century when it was featured in several reputable cookbooks, including those by Fannie Farmer, and became a holiday staple that is still cherished today. In fact, November 27 is recognized annually as National Bavarian Cream Pie Day! ✦ *Makes 8 servings*

FOR THE PIE CRUST
1 cup (120 g) all-purpose flour
½ teaspoon (2.5 g) salt
⅓ cup (75 g) unsalted butter, frozen
    and grated
3 tablespoons (45 mL) cold water
3 tablespoons (15 g) sweetened coconut
    flakes, lightly toasted

FOR THE FILLING
1 (¼-ounce/42 g) packet unflavored
    gelatin
½ cup (100 g) sugar
½ teaspoon (2.5 g) salt

¼ cup (60 mL) cold water
4 large eggs, separated
1 cup (240 mL) milk
1 cup (240 mL) heavy cream
½ teaspoon (1 g) freshly grated nutmeg

FOR THE COCONUT CHANTILLY CREAM
½ cup (120 mL) heavy cream
3 tablespoons (36 g) confectioners' sugar
1 teaspoon (5 mL) vanilla bean paste
½ teaspoon (2.5 g) salt
¼ cup (17 g) sweetened coconut flakes,
    lightly toasted
Shaved dark chocolate, for garnish

*Recipe continues* ➤

1. Preheat the oven to 450°F (230°C).

2. To make the pie crust, sift together the flour and salt into a food processor, then add the butter and coconut. Pulse several times while slowly drizzling in the cold water through the feed tube until the dough just begins to form a ball. Transfer to a bowl and refrigerate for 30 minutes to hydrate the dough and chill the butter.

3. Roll the dough out to about $\frac{1}{4}$-inch thickness. Place the dough in a 9-inch pie pan, pressing it gently into the corners. Prick the base of the pie crust several times with a fork and bake until golden brown, 10 to 12 minutes. Set aside to cool.

4. To make the filling, combine the gelatin, $\frac{1}{4}$ cup of the sugar, salt, and cold water in a small bowl. Mix and allow the gelatin to bloom for about 5 minutes.

5. Pour an inch or two of water into a medium saucepan and bring to a boil. In a heatproof bowl, combine the egg yolks, milk, bloomed gelatin, and $\frac{1}{2}$ cup of the heavy cream. Whisk until the custard thickens and can coat the back of a spoon, 5 to 7 minutes. Remove the bowl and set aside to cool.

6. In a bowl or stand mixer, beat the egg whites to nearly stiff peaks. Gradually add the remaining $\frac{1}{4}$ cup sugar 1 tablespoon at a time until the meringue is silky and has stiff peaks. Fold the whipped cream into the cooled custard mixture. Whip the remaining $\frac{1}{2}$ cup heavy cream and fold into the mixture, along with the nutmeg. Pour the mixture into the cooled pie shell, level with an offset spatula, and refrigerate until set, about 6 hours or overnight.

7. To make the coconut Chantilly cream, whip the heavy cream to stiff peaks with the confectioners' sugar, vanilla, salt, and coconut. Top the pie with the coconut Chantilly cream or simply some freshly shaved dark chocolate. Serve immediately.

# CHOCOLATE CRUNCH PIE

THE classic chocolate custard pie has always made me smile from ear to ear: There's something about it that ticks every box when I'm craving something sweet and chocolaty. One day, while reading through some old recipes from the 1970s, I came across this gem of a dessert. It was from one of my favorite types of cookbooks: church community cookbooks, with their spiral-bound covers and brief bios of the women that were adding their favorite recipes for all to enjoy. Thumbing through, I found this particular treat, calling for crushed Oreo cookies for the crust rather than graham cracker crumbs. I loved it because it was quick and convenient to make, as many of the recipes that came from the late 1960s and '70s were built around convenience, like using packaged products or the microwave for basically everything. After one bite, I knew it would quickly become a favorite of mine.

The richness of this custardy chocolate pie is perfectly balanced by velvety whipped cream, which is lightly enhanced with a hint of salt. The ground pecans add a wonderful nuttiness to the pie, but it tastes just as good without them—or with any other crunchy component you prefer.

This pie is best served cold, and unlike revenge, sharing this recipe is sure to make you new friends! ✦ *Makes 8 servings*

### FOR THE PIE CRUST
- 2 cups (250 g) crushed Oreo cookie crumbs (from about 22 Oreos; see Note)
- 5 tablespoons (70 g) unsalted butter, melted
- ⅛ teaspoon (0.6 g) salt

### FOR THE CHOCOLATE FILLING
- 5 large egg yolks
- 1½ cups (300 g) sugar
- ¼ cup (30 g) cornstarch
- ¼ teaspoon (2 g) salt

- 3 cups (700 mL) whole milk
- 6½ ounces (184 g) semisweet chocolate, finely chopped
- 2 teaspoons (10 mL) vanilla bean paste
- 2 tablespoons (28 g) unsalted butter

### FOR THE TOPPING
- 1 cup (240 mL) heavy cream
- ¼ cup (30 g) confectioners' sugar
- Pinch salt
- 1 teaspoon (5 mL) vanilla bean paste
- ½ cup (65 g) ground pecans (optional)
- Chocolate shavings, for garnish (optional)

1. Preheat the oven to 350°F (175°C).

2. To make the pie crust, put the Oreo cookie crumbs in a bowl and fold in the melted butter and salt—it will appear to be wet. Transfer the mixture to a 9-inch pie pan and firmly pack the crumbs into the bottom and sides using the bottom of a measuring cup. Bake for 10 to 12 minutes. Allow to cool completely.

*Recipe continues* ➤

3. To make the chocolate filling, put the egg yolks in a heatproof bowl. Combine the sugar, cornstarch, salt, and milk in a medium saucepan and cook over medium heat for 3 to 5 minutes, until the sugar has dissolved and the mixture begins to mildly scald. Remove from the heat and ladle some of the warm liquid into the egg yolks, whisking to prevent them from scrambling. Once the eggs have tempered, pour them into the warm milk mixture, return to the medium heat and cook for 8 to 10 minutes while whisking constantly. The mixture will begin to thicken, like a rich pudding. Remove from the heat when thick enough to coat the back of a spoon. Fold in the chopped chocolate, vanilla, and butter. Mix thoroughly.

4. Pour the filling into the cooled pie crust and refrigerate for several hours, until it has fully cooled and set.

5. When ready to serve, make the topping: Whip the cream to stiff peaks with the confectioners' sugar, salt, and vanilla. Cover the surface of the pie with the whipped cream and top with the ground pecans and chocolate shavings, if you like. Serve chilled.

**NOTE:** *To crush the Oreo cookies, pulse them in a food processor until finely crushed and uniform.*

# ESSENTIALS, EXTRAS & EVERYDAY SKILLS

**THIS** chapter is short and straightforward, packed with essential information that I believe everyone should know while exploring this book. Each item represents a simple technique or recipe that can enhance anyone's cooking experience. Many of these skills might've been considered essential around the turn of the twentieth century, and were usually taught from parent to child, but many were lost during turbulent times, when there were more pressing issues to attend to—like finding your next meal. By the 1950s, generations had passed, and many were lacking these once-common skills, which I think contributed to the reliance on convenience foods that took over from the 1960s onward.

For example, learning how to make stock will not only save you *so much* money in the long run but will also improve the flavor of your dishes. Understanding what a cartouche is, along with when and how to use one, will significantly elevate your cooking and keep your dishes covered and moist. Addi-

tionally, I've included smaller tips and tricks to assist you in a pinch, such as how to make brown sugar when you find yourself running low, and a number of simple, delicious sauces and condiments that you'll soon learn to whip up in less time than it takes to make some toast.

While there could easily be dozens of additional tips to include, I believe these key points will be sufficient to empower you to create the best recipes as you journey through the decades of cooking.

# SAUCE VELOUTÉ

◇◇◇◇◇◇◇◇◇◇◇◇◇◇◇◇◇◇◇◇◇◇◇◇◇◇ **1810s** ◇◇◇◇◇◇◇◇◇◇◇◇◇◇◇◇◇◇◇◇◇◇◇

ONE of the five "mother sauces" created and named by the legendary French chef Auguste Escoffier, velouté is one of the easiest to make, and its applications are nearly endless. In fact, many of the sauces you'll encounter in this book are variations of a simple velouté sauce. The French word *velouté* literally translates to "velvety," which perfectly describes the rich, creamy texture this sauce adds to countless dishes—like a warm, flavorful hug. While that might sound somewhat dramatic, its deliciousness and simplicity make it a fantastic option.

This is the baseline to create a simple velouté, but let your imagination and your recipes dictate what you add to it. For instance, you can infuse the velouté with fresh herbs, like thyme or rosemary, or add aromatics, like shallots or garlic. So, stop buying canned cream-of-something soup and let's get cooking! ✦ *Makes 1½ cups*

| | |
|---|---|
| 2 tablespoons (28 g) unsalted butter | 2 cups (480 mL) Homemade Chicken |
| 2 tablespoons (16 g) plus 1 teaspoon | Stock (page 225), cold |
| (3 g) all-purpose flour | Salt to taste |
| | Freshly grated nutmeg |

1. In a medium saucepan, melt the butter over medium-low heat. Add the flour and whisk until it thickens up in the fat. Continue to cook for 3 to 5 minutes to cook out the rawness of the flour.

2. When the roux begins to gently tan and small bubbles are forming, add the cold stock. Turn the heat up to medium-high and whisk constantly as the liquid begins to absorb into the roux.

3. When the sauce has the consistency of honey as it falls from a spoon, you're approaching the right texture. If you continue to reduce this you'll have a thicker sauce, with a more concentrated flavor. I generally stop when I dip a spoon into the sauce and I can sweep my finger across the back of the spoon and a clean streak is left behind without running together. This stage is called *nappé*. It will take 5 to 7 minutes all together.

4. Season with salt and a pinch of freshly grated nutmeg. Serve warm.

**TIPS FOR SAUCES:**

*A roux can be made using any fat with flour, like butter, olive oil, rendered bacon fat, or margarine.*

*It is best practice to introduce cold liquid into the hot roux. This will prevent clumping in the flour and will result in the finest sauces.*

*You can keep the sauce warm by keeping it in a heatproof tumbler or in a bain marie, in which you submerge the entire vessel in warm water to keep it from reducing more or cooling too much.*

BUTTER >

\+

< FLOUR

STOCK >

< NUTMEG

=

BUTTER  >

<  FLOUR

+

COLD MILK  >

<  NUTMEG

=

# SAUCE BÉCHAMEL

◇◇◇◇◇◇◇◇◇◇◇◇◇◇◇◇◇◇◇◇◇◇◇◇◇◇◇◇◇◇ **1730s** ◇◇◇◇◇◇◇◇◇◇◇◇◇◇◇◇◇◇◇◇◇◇◇◇◇◇◇◇◇◇

ANOTHER of the five "mother sauces" created by Auguste Escoffier, béchamel is essentially the exact same as Sauce Velouté (page 216) but has a creamier quality with the substitution of milk for the stock. Often referred to as simply "white sauce," béchamel is one of the most versatile sauces, as it brings a creaminess to almost any dish without disrupting the flavors of everything else.

This is the baseline to create a simple béchamel, but let your imagination and your recipes dictate what you add to it. One of the easiest ways to impart more flavor to the béchamel is to infuse the milk with herbs, like thyme or rosemary, or aromatics, like shallots or garlic. The milk will absorb the flavors of most ingredients. If you heat the milk with aromatics, allow the milk to cool completely before adding it to the roux. You'll often see a béchamel sauce used in Southern American gravies for dishes like biscuits and gravy. If you whisk an egg yolk into the sauce as it's warm (not hot), then you make an "enriched" béchamel, which is perfect for lasagna or a traditional moussaka.

✦ *Makes 1½ cups*

| | |
|---|---|
| 2 tablespoons (28 g) unsalted butter | 2 cups (480 mL) milk, cold |
| 2 tablespoons (16 g) plus 1 teaspoon (3 g) all-purpose flour | Salt to taste |
| | Freshly grated nutmeg |

1. In a medium saucepan, melt the butter over medium-low heat. Add the flour and whisk until it thickens up in the fat. Continue to cook for 3 to 5 minutes until the rawness of the flour is cooked out.

2. When the roux begins to gently tan and small bubbles are forming, add the cold milk. Turn the heat up to medium-high and whisk constantly as the milk begins to absorb into the roux.

3. When the sauce has the consistency of a thin mayonnaise, you're approaching the right texture. If you continue to reduce this you'll have a thicker sauce, with a more concentrated flavor. I generally stop when I dip a spoon into the sauce and I can sweep my finger across the back of the spoon and a clean streak is left behind without running together. This stage is called *nappé*. It will take 5 to 7 minutes all together.

4. Season with salt and a pinch of freshly grated nutmeg. Serve warm.

# SAUCE SUPRÊME

◇◇◇◇◇◇◇◇◇◇◇◇◇◇◇◇◇◇◇◇◇◇◇◇ **1930s** ◇◇◇◇◇◇◇◇◇◇◇◇◇◇◇◇◇◇◇◇◇◇◇◇

ALONG with the five "mother sauces" established by Auguste Escoffier, there are numerous "daughter sauces" that build upon the foundation of the mother sauces by incorporating additional ingredients or techniques. For instance, some daughter sauces may include wine, mushrooms, or a combination of multiple sauces to enhance the final flavor of the dish.

One of my favorite sauces to prepare is sauce suprême. This sauce enhances Sauce Velouté (page 216) with heavy cream, creating a superior (or "supreme") sauce that is perfect for adding creaminess to almost any dish. ✦ *Makes 1½ cups*

2 tablespoons (28 g) unsalted butter
2 tablespoons (16 g) plus 1 teaspoon
  (3 g) all-purpose flour
1½ cups (360 mL) Homemade Chicken
  Stock (page 225), cold

½ cup (120 mL) heavy cream, cold
Salt to taste
Freshly grated nutmeg

1. In a medium saucepan, melt the butter over medium-low heat. Add the flour and whisk until it thickens up in the fat. Continue to cook for 3 to 5 minutes until the rawness of the flour is cooked out.

2. When the roux begins to gently tan and small bubbles are forming, add the cold stock. Turn the heat up to medium-high and whisk constantly as the liquid begins to absorb into the roux.

3. When the sauce has the consistency of honey as it falls from a spoon, add the heavy cream and continue to slowly reduce. I generally stop when I dip a spoon into the sauce and I can sweep my finger across the back of the spoon and a clean streak is left behind without running together. This stage is called *nappé*. It will take 5 to 7 minutes all together.

4. Season with salt and a pinch of freshly grated nutmeg. Serve warm.

BUTTER >

FLOUR >

+

STOCK >

<

HEAVY
CREAM

=

△ NUTMEG

EGGS >

< OIL

MUSTARD >

+

< VINEGAR

SALT >

=

# MAYONNAISE

I F you've followed my channel long enough, you'll know that I actually loathe mayonnaise in most applications. Perhaps it's just from growing up with a large jar of Miracle Whip sitting in my fridge, but the look, smell, and even the taste were just never there for me. But as I got older, and as I started working in kitchens, I learned that making your own mayonnaise is incredibly easy and it *tastes better*!

Until the beginning of the 1900s, mayonnaise was simply a condiment that was made at home, when a recipe called for a creamy element. It wasn't until Mrs. Schlorer's started jarring their commercially made mayo in 1907 that the condiment craze started to take off. Shortly after, Richard Hellmann, the owner of a delicatessen in New York, started to package his famous mayonnaise, which quickly became the standard for millions. We can likely thank the 1960s for ruining this condiment for me, as this was a time of—ahem—creative experimentation. With the advent of "low-fat foods" and nobody to bounce ideas off of, we were soon adding mayo to everything, from sandwiches to anything gelatin. Oh, how we lost our way.

This mayonnaise recipe is so simple, but it does model itself closer to a Japanese style of mayonnaise, which is enriched with additional egg yolks and a pinch of MSG. Add garlic, chiles, or herbs for an easy and tasty way to improve upon your sauce. ✦ *Makes 1 cup*

1 large egg (50 g) plus 1 large egg yolk (18 g)
1 tablespoon (15 g) Dijon mustard
1 tablespoon (15 mL) white wine vinegar
¼ teaspoon (1.5 g) fine sea salt, or more to taste

Pinch MSG
1 cup (240 mL) olive oil or vegetable oil
1 teaspoon (5 mL) fresh lemon juice (optional)

1. If using a food processor, add the egg, egg yolk, mustard, vinegar, salt, and MSG to the food processor, turn it on, and slowly start adding the oil through the feed tube. Begin with drops of oil at a time until it begins to emulsify, and then you can gradually add a slow, steady stream of oil until the mayonnaise is complete.

2. If making the mayonnaise by hand in a bowl, do the same thing but wrap a damp tea towel around the base of the bowl. As you're whisking and pouring the oil, the towel will help keep the bowl in place, rather than it rolling around, as tends to happen when you don't have the extra hand to hold the bowl down.

3. Taste and adjust the seasoning. Add more salt or a squeeze of lemon juice, if you'd like a bit more acid.

**NOTE:** *I use mayonnaise when grilling bread, rather than oil or butter, because it makes the best grilled cheeses and toasted sandwiches! Simply spread some across the bread, assemble and bake in the oven for a golden, zingy, and perfectly toasty sando.*

# FLORIDA OLD SOUR

AS a Floridian, I love the old history that this state has. From the earliest settlers to the proximity of the Caribbean, Florida has a rich history with the sea. One popular condiment, called old sour, can be found in the Florida Keys and Caribbean and was at one time as ubiquitous on a table as ketchup or mustard.

Historically, the concept of utilizing fermented ingredients like sauerkraut or kimchi as condiments is nothing new, though it's not practiced as commonly in the States as in other parts of the world. Before the invention of the refrigerator, most ingredients utilized methods of preservation to extend shelf life for whole seasons, such as using salt to cure proteins or pickling a vegetable to keep it crisp and edible months later.

As simple as it is, old sour packs a punch when dashed on soups or stews, added to your eggs, or even with your favorite fried treats. Being a fermented product, it offers a funky depth, with the sweet, bright acid of key limes, the saltiness to round out your palate, and the back heat of a Scotch bonnet pepper. It's a labor of love, since you'll be waiting at least two weeks before you can use it, but it'll never spoil and will last a long time before you need to make another batch. ✦ *Makes 1 cup*

1 cup (240 mL) fresh key lime juice (from about 2 dozen key limes)

2 teaspoons (6 g) kosher salt

1 Scotch bonnet pepper, quartered (including seeds)

1. In a bowl, combine the lime juice and salt and mix to incorporate and dissolve the salt. Add the Scotch bonnet pepper, cover, and marinate overnight in the refrigerator.

2. Strain out the lime pulp, pepper, and seeds and return the juice to a sterilized glass jar.

3. Leave at room temperature in a dark space for at least 2 weeks to ferment. It will keep indefinitely and is shelf stable, even after it's been opened.

**NOTE:** *Old sour is safe to consume as a fermented product. Ensure your storage jars are sterilized before adding the juice to avoid mold and bad bacterial growth.*

# HOMEMADE CHICKEN STOCK

**1700s**

"IF you know, you know" is one of the most appropriate sayings when it comes to homemade ingredients like chicken stock. For years I would simply run to the store, buy some shelf-stable boxed broth, and cook with it. It's fine. It gets the job done. But if you're looking to have heads turn, eyes widen, and people call you "chef" when they eat your dishes, then homemade is the way to go.

This recipe is incredibly simple but offers a massive pack of goodness. Chicken wings and chicken feet are essential ingredients that are going to give your stock the quintessential mouthfeel that we expect from a good stock. Roasting them and slowly simmering for hours will denature the collagen-rich cuts into gelatin, which is essential when making a delicious soup or sauce.

This stock is not seasoned with any salt or pepper, as a stock should be neutral.

✦ *Makes 10 quarts*

2 chicken carcasses
1 pound (450 g) chicken feet
1 pound (450 g) chicken wings
2 tablespoons (30 g) tomato paste
3 onions, quartered
3 carrots, roughly chopped

3 celery stalks, roughly chopped
4 garlic cloves, crushed
2 fresh parsley sprigs
4 fresh thyme sprigs
12 quarts (12 L) water

1. Preheat the oven to 400°F (200°C).

2. In a large roasting pan, rub the chicken carcasses, feet, and wings with the tomato paste. Add the onions, carrots, and celery and roast for 30 minutes, or until dark tan but not burnt.

3. Transfer the roasted chicken and vegetables to a very large stockpot. Add the garlic, parsley, thyme, and water and bring to a boil, then immediately turn the heat down to medium-low.

4. Simmer for 3 hours, skimming the surface of the stock for impurities, foam, and fat.

5. Carefully strain the stock through a chinois or a colander lined with cheesecloth, or filter the stock several times through a fine-mesh strainer.

6. Allow to cool completely, then transfer to airtight containers. Store in the refrigerator for up to 1 week or in the freezer for up to 6 months.

**NOTES:** *If you don't want to make your own chicken stock, a good trick is to simply add a packet of unflavored gelatin to store-bought stock. This will give the needed mouthfeel that you lose from the box stuff.*

*I never really make beef stock because I prefer the taste and lightness that chicken stock gives my dishes, but you can make your own beef stock by following this template, roasting a lot of bones and simmering the stock for 4 to 6 hours.*

# CARTOUCHE

KNOWN as a "false lid," a cartouche is a chef's best friend. Whether I'm making a braised dish, preparing stock, or baking a cake in a springform pan, a cartouche is essential. The applications for this simple culinary technique are extensive and limited only by your creativity.

In essence, a cartouche is just a paper lid that covers pots and pans. So, why does it deserve its own section in this book? Because once you understand evaporation, you'll never look back.

When cooking in a pot, Dutch oven, or even a pan, liquids will evaporate when exposed to heat. In many dishes, this is a desirable effect—we want to reduce liquids to concentrate flavors, enhance the mouthfeel of sauces, or simply keep something warm, which leads to the gradual loss of liquid. However, when braising, the distance between the proteins being cooked and the metal lid of a Dutch oven may span 4 to 6 inches. This distance can cause proteins to dry out more quickly, resulting in tough and unpleasant food after hours of cooking.

By using a cartouche and fitting it on top of the liquid, you can significantly reduce this distance, allowing liquid to evaporate while still self-basting the food. This technique results in incredibly tender dishes.

Are you baking cakes? A cartouche can also help ensure that your cake does not stick to the bottom of the pan. Simply create a cartouche base for the pan, pour the batter on top, and the risk of sticking is virtually eliminated.

I could go on about this topic, but you get the point. This simple skill is not only easy to master but will also impress your friends when you showcase it in your cooking.

1. Fold a large sheet of parchment paper in half, then in half again the other way. Make sure the folds are as clean as possible.

2. With the folded corner at the bottom, fold the rectangle in half on the diagonal to form a triangle. Repeat to make a smaller triangle, and repeat again until you have a tight "paper airplane" shape.

3. Bring the point of the cartouche to the center of any circular pot or pan and cut the paper at the spot where it reaches the rim of the pan. This will dictate the diameter of the cartouche and will make it a perfect fit every time. Snip a small tiny bit off the tip of the point. Unfold the cartouche and use as a lid or liner for a cake pan.

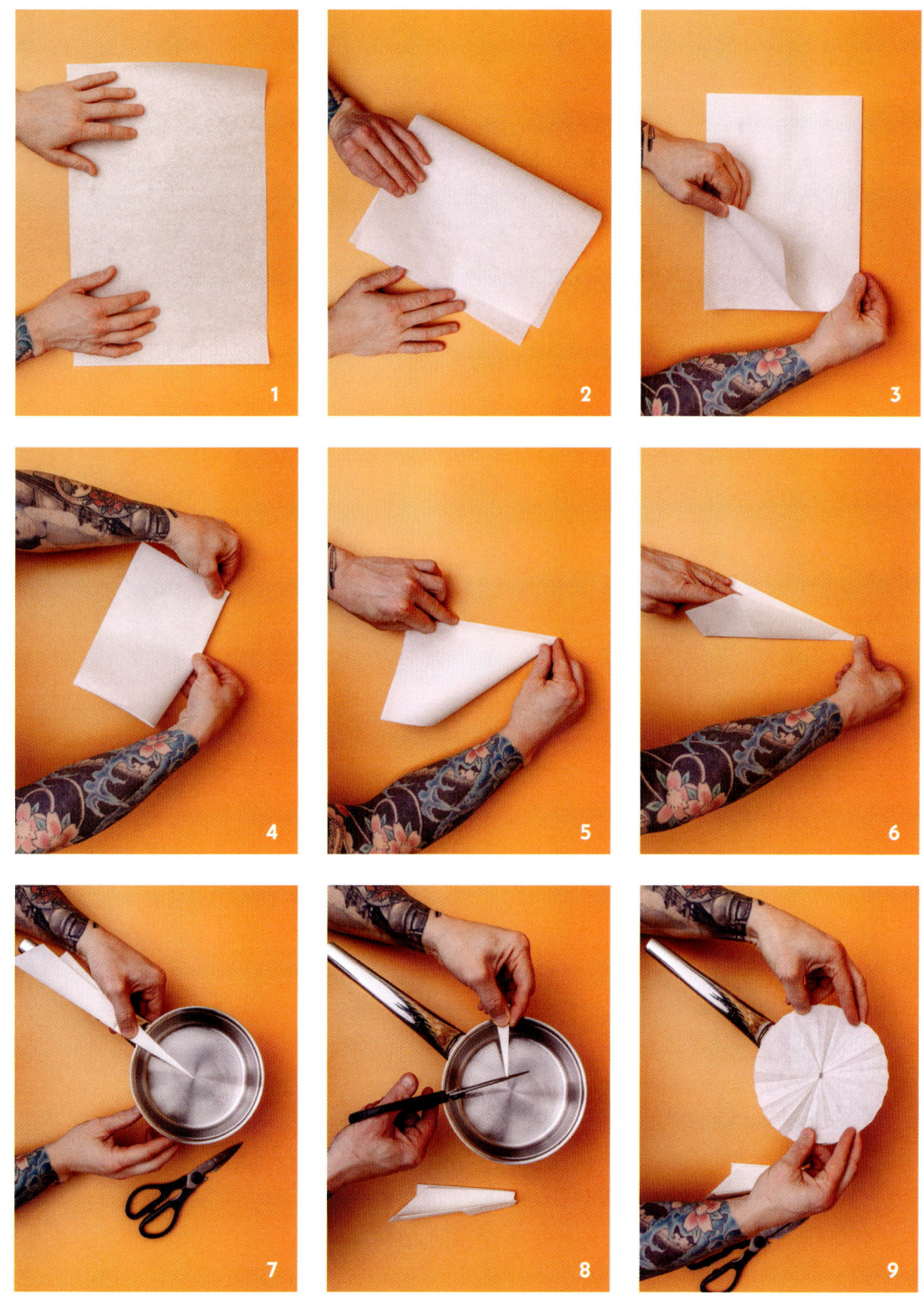

# BROWN SUGAR

THERE are few things more annoying than running out of eggs or brown sugar in the middle of a recipe. Though I can't help much with the availability, cost, or abundance of eggs, I can help with this simple and essential trick so you never run out of brown sugar again. ✦ *Makes 1 cup*

| 1 cup (200 g) sugar | 1 tablespoon (21 g) molasses |
|---|---|

In a bowl, combine the sugar and molasses and whisk until completely incorporated and a light brown color. Use right away or transfer to an airtight container for storage.

**NOTE:** *This recipe will make light brown sugar. To make dark brown sugar, simply double up on the molasses.*

# BOUQUET GARNI

**1600s**

**WHEN** making a delicious soup, stew, or stock, you want to impart as much flavor as possible, and with the help of a few herbs and peppercorns you'll be calling "hands" at the pass while you're feeding all of your family and friends. Traditionally, a bouquet garni of herbs is tied between a couple dark leek greens, but I love the convenience and reliability of tea sachets. I can fill them with a lot more, without the fuss of keeping everything together as in the classic method. ✦ *Makes 1 sachet*

4 to 6 fresh parsley sprigs
4 to 6 fresh thyme sprigs
2 bay leaves

2 tablespoons (14 g) black peppercorns,
   roughly crushed

Stack the parsley and thyme stems on top of the bay leaves and add to a tea sachet, along with the peppercorns. (Alternatively, place the ingredients in a square of cheesecloth and tie together with twine.)

# PASTRY CREAM

WHEN we think of sweets, we usually think of cookies, cakes, pies, and things of that nature. But I think a *really good* sweet treat should have some custard in it.

Fruit tarts, pies, éclairs, Boston cream doughnuts—I can go on—all incorporate a very special type of custard that we call "pastry cream," also known as crème pâtissière. This versatile and delicious custard can be flavored in almost any way and is thicker, like a pudding, rather than a loose custard like crème anglaise.

It does require a bit of patience and a lot of focus, but it's well worth mastering this simple technique, and with the steps below, I think you'll do just fine. ✦ *Makes 2½ cups*

| | |
|---|---|
| 2 cups (455 g) whole milk | ¼ teaspoon kosher salt |
| Seeds scraped from 1 vanilla bean | 4 large egg yolks |
| ½ cup (100 g) sugar | 2 tablespoons (28 g) unsalted butter, cut |
| 3 tablespoons (30 g) cornstarch | into small cubes |

1. In a medium saucepan over medium-high heat, combine the milk and vanilla seeds. Bring to a simmer, then reduce the heat, cover, and simmer for 30 minutes. Check periodically to ensure it's not reducing or burning, but just simmering gently.

2. In a small bowl, combine the sugar, cornstarch, salt, and egg yolks and whisk until the mixture has a pale yellow color and a silky, fluffy texture.

3. Gently pour one-quarter of the warm vanilla-infused milk into the egg mixture and rapidly whisk for 30 seconds to temper the eggs. Then pour the egg mixture into the pan and turn the heat up to medium. Cook, whisking often, until the mixture begins to thicken slightly and you begin to see a "burp" of bubbles, 5 to 7 minutes. At that point, continuously whisk for an additional 1 minute. Remove from the heat.

4. Add the cold cubes of butter, whisking after each addition until fully incorporated.

5. Strain the cream through a fine-mesh strainer or chinois into a bowl. Press a piece of plastic wrap down on the surface of the cream to prevent a skin from forming. Place the bowl in a larger bowl of ice water to rapidly cool the custard for 10 minutes, then transfer to the refrigerator.

6. Once cool, the pastry cream will be very thick. You can loosen it a bit with a whisk and then transfer to a piping bag or other container for your desired presentation.

# CHOUX PASTRY

OF all the wonderful delicacies the French have given to the world, perhaps my favorite is choux pastry, also known as pâte à choux.

Choux (pronounced like "shoe") is one of the most versatile and flavorful doughs, in my opinion. While it requires a bit of technique, speed, and skill to master, once you understand the process, you'll consistently achieve great results.

Making choux pastry is different from preparing most other batters, where you simply mix the ingredients in a bowl. Instead, this French recipe involves a bit of cooking. You start by boiling water and milk with butter, then quickly add flour to the pan while stirring. Next, you incorporate eggs, resulting in a gluey, sticky dough that is best handled with a pastry bag, as it can be unwieldy otherwise.

This single batter is incredibly versatile! You can use it to make éclairs, profiteroles (cream puffs), churros, beignets, doughnuts, gougères, Parisienne gnocchi, and many more delicious treats. It can be steamed, boiled, baked, or fried—truly, it is my favorite dough in the world! ✦ *Makes about 1½ cups*

| | |
|---|---|
| ½ cup (120 g) water | ½ teaspoon (2 g) kosher salt |
| ½ cup (120 g) milk | 1 cup (120 g) all-purpose flour, sifted |
| 6 tablespoons (84 g) unsalted butter | 4 large eggs (200 g), beaten |
| 2 teaspoons (10 g) sugar | |

1. Combine the water, milk, butter, sugar, and salt in a medium saucepan and bring to a boil.

2. Once the liquid is boiling and the butter has fully melted, remove from the heat and add all the flour at once, immediately mixing with a silicone spatula to form a dough. Mix until there are no lumps of flour.

3. Return the pan to medium-low heat and continue to beat the dough until a thin skin forms on the bottom of the pot. The dough temperature should be somewhere between 165 and 175°F (74–79°C). Remove from the heat.

4. At this stage you can transfer the dough to a stand mixer fitted with the paddle attachment or mix by hand. Add the beaten eggs in four portions, mixing thoroughly after each addition. At first it may appear that the mixture is "broken," but it will eventually come together as a rich dough.

5. Transfer the dough to a piping bag fitted with the tip you'd like to use.

**NOTES:** *You can store the dough in an airtight container in the refrigerator for up to 3 days or in the freezer for up to 3 months.*

*This dough is also perfect for savory applications like Parisienne gnocchi; simply omit the sugar and replace with chopped fresh herbs or grated cheese.*

# ACKNOWLEDGMENTS

**THIS** book, love it or hate it, is the culmination of years of research, trial and error, and a mild neurodivergent hyperfixation. My love of history, food, and the art of cooking is something I've been workshopping for over a decade, and it took friends and family suggesting the idea of a book to plant the seed and grow into this finished product.

I am incredibly proud of what I've done, and I can promise you it was harder than you'd ever imagine to select one hundred recipes out of the thousands that I've read. It has taken months of testing, conceptualizing, and doubting myself, scrambling to meet deadlines, and constantly wondering if what I'm doing is enough. I truly hope it *is* enough.

I hope that you thumb through these pages, make these dishes, and improve upon them with your own touches! That is truly the essence of cooking. It is knowing enough to start and finish a dish, and knowing enough to understand how you'd make it better for your own palate—or for your family.

I want to thank so many people for their time, their love, and their trust in the creation of this book. Without these people, this wouldn't be more than just an idea, and for me that would've been enough. I've never been the best at championing myself, and it literally took a village of amazing folks to lift me up and help me push this from an idea into reality.

Firstly, thanks to Keiko, my partner and love of my life. You were the first one there when I needed you and were always the loudest voice of support when the idea of a book came up. Your

style, vision, and creativity balance mine in a way that always elevates anything I do, even if I'm slow to get around to it. Without you, this book wouldn't have the beautiful images and wonderful suggestions to improve many of these retro recipes. I would be an entirely different person without you in my life, and you make me better and make me want to be better every day. I love you more than living itself and couldn't do this without you.

A massive thanks to my amazing literary agent, Amanda Bernardi, who had my back from day one and believed in my insane idea to create a book about recipes from a hundred years ago or more. Your kindness and genuine interest in this

233

process have been so helpful, and it was always amazing knowing I had you in my corner.

To Ann, Allison, and the incredible team at Countryman Press, thank you for taking a chance on a tattooed nerd who loves to cook. This book was truly made possible because you believed in me and felt the passion I had behind my eyes. Working with you all has been the most difficult and rewarding thing I've done in too long, and I'm the better for it.

To my *incredible* illustrator, Brandon Campbell, thank you, sir. As someone who had already loved your work for quite some time, it's a wholly different experience knowing that you helped bring this book to life. I truly wouldn't have wanted (and couldn't have asked for) a better partner with the visual journey, and I cannot wait to get some of these pieces tattooed on my body. When we eventually meet, there will be many hugs.

To my family—I love you all. My brother, Ben, is quietly one of my strongest supporters, but someone that I know I've made proud. I know that our parents are slow-clapping somewhere right now, in the Great Beyond.

To my best friend, Billy—you have always been my other brother, my big brother. You've looked out for me since we were teenagers, making questionable late-night decisions, cruising the streets, listening to metal *way* too loudly. There are so many people that I know support me, but you are my ride-or-die, and even if we don't see each other as often as we'd like, it always feels like we pick up where we left off, and always will. I love you, brother.

To Amanda Fiske and the rest of Keiko's incredible family: Thank you for believing in me *way* before I believed in myself. You have always seen something in me that I couldn't but helped lift me up to get there, and I wouldn't be here without your love, time, and creativity. You have

been my family since day one, and I will always be here for you.

And to Michelle Fiske, thank you for being one of the most supportive people and the best recipe tester I could've reached out to. You have been in my corner, cheering me on, and were the first person I thought of when I needed to test these treats. Thank you for always being such an amazing friend and family member.

And to the *many* individual friends who have shaped me into the person that I am today—thank you. It's impossible to encapsulate all the influence and support I've received in my life in some short blurb, and if you know me, you also know that I've likely told you recently how important you are to me, given you a hug, or thanked you.

Lastly, thank *you*. If you purchased this book, you've likely been supporting my work for years, but even if you just discovered me recently or received this book as a gift, just know that I am and will always be here to thank you. If you ever see me in person, please stop and say hello (I mean it!). Please let me know if any of these recipes made you happy or sparked some food memory because I would not even have this opportunity if it wasn't for you and the others who took the time to support my work. I hope to be doing this for a long time because I'm doing this for you.

I hope this isn't the last opportunity that I'll have to create a book, but I am beyond proud in this moment, and that is enough for now.

# INDEX

Note: Page references in *italics* indicate photographs.